God Thoughts

52 Week Devotional

Destiny Green

God thoughts

God Thoughts: 52 Week Devotional

Copyright © 2024 by Destiny Green

Printed in the United States of America

ISBN: 979-8-218-40900-5 (Paperback)

Published by: Joseph's Ministry, LLC

www.josephsministryllc.com

Scripture quotations marked (GNT) are from the Good News Translation in Today's English Version- Second Edition Copyright© 1992 by American Bible Society. Used by Permission.

Scripture quotations marked (NIV) are taken from THE HOLY BIBLE, NEW INTERNATIONAL VERSION®. Copyright© 1973, 1978, 1984, 2011 by Biblica, Inc.™. Used by permission of Zondervan.

Scripture quotations marked (NKJV) are taken from the NEW KING JAMES VERSION®. Copyright© 1982 by Thomas Nelson, Inc. Used by permission. All rights reserved.

Scripture quotations marked (Amp) are taken from the AMPLIFIED® BIBLE, Copyright© 1954, 1958, 1962, 1964, 1965, 1987 by the Lockman Foundation. Used by Permission. (www.Lockman.org)

Scripture quotations marked (NLT) are taken from the Holy Bible, New Living Translation, copyright©1996, 2004, 2015 by Tyndale House Foundation. Used by permission of Tyndale House Publishers, Carol Stream, Illinois 60188. All rights reserved.

Scripture quotations marked (NCV) are taken from the NEW CENTURY VERSION®. Copyright© 2005 by Thomas Nelson, Inc. Used by permission. All rights reserved.

Scripture quotations marked MSG are taken from THE MESSAGE, copyright© 1993, 2002, 2018 by Eugene H. Peterson. Used by permission of NavPress, represented by Tyndale House Publishers. All rights reserved.

Scripture quotations marked (KJV) are taken from the KING JAMES VERSION, public domain.

ALL RIGHTS RESERVED. Printed in the United States of America. No part of this book may be used or reproduced in any manner whatsoever without written permission from the author except in the case of brief quotations embodied in critical articles or reviews.

This Journal Belongs To

———————————————

From

———————————————

Table of Contents

Introduction 3

God's Thoughts 5

Vision 9

God Is Concerned About The Things You Are Concerned About .. 13

I'm Hurting 17

Will You Give God The Opportunity? 21

Enjoying Your Life 25

Eight Dimensions To Wellness 29

God's Faithfulness 33

He Lifted My Bowed Down Head 37

Keep Your Word To Yourself 41

Vices That Hinder Purpose 45

Do You Have Unforgiveness Lingering In Your Heart? .. 49

Loving Others That Have Wronged You 53

Judging Others 57

Pray For The Women and Children 61

Pray For The Women and Children Part 2 65

Seasons In Life 69

Defeating Goliaths In Your Life 73

All Things Will Work Together For Your Good 77

Get Busy 81

Wayward Children 85

We Have Free Will 89

Generosity 93

Betrayal 97

What's the Reason For The Hope You Have? 101

Don't Be Afraid Of Rejection 105

God Doesn't Show Favoritism 109

Miracle Moments 113

Pursuing God 117

Resolve It	121
Access Granted	125
God's Love For Us Never Fails	129
Moving Forward	133
Preserving Tradition	137
Our Speech Matters	141
How Does God Feel About How We Utilize Our Time?	145
Caregiving	149
Bye Bye Fear	153
Spiritual Warfare	157
Live An Honest Life	161
Broken Hearted	165
We Are Protected	169
Lies We Believe	173
Rules and Consequences	177
Freedom	181
Persistence	185
Injustice	189
Living Beyond Your Emotions	193
Encourage Yourself	197
A Thankful Attitude	201
Purposed	205
Benediction	209
About the Author	213

I want to thank my Heavenly Father for allowing me to write this devotional and all who have supported me by purchasing a copy for themselves or others. I thank my mom, Juanita Green, for introducing me to God and teaching me the importance of acknowledging and serving Him. I thank my godmother, Cecilia Lott, for nurturing my spiritual walk with Christ and allowing my gifts to be stirred under her leadership. I'm most thankful for my first church home, Christ Temple Baptist Church, founded by Rev. William S. and Anna Hill. They were so instrumental in my walk with Christ. I appreciate them for nurturing and protecting my gifts as a child. They handled all the children in the ministry with care. I want to thank my neighbor mom, Verlean Andrews, for affirming my boldness, courage, and gift of singing. She would always call my mother and request my sister and me to her home to sing for her company and would be overjoyed. May Rev. William S. and Anna Hill and Verlean Andrews RIH.

Love y'all always!

Introduction

Do you have a hard time focusing on how to read the bible? Is it hard for you to find what book to start reading? Trying to understand scripture can be intimidating, but it can also be enlightening. Whether you are new to the Bible or seeking to deepen your understanding of the Bible, God Thoughts provides real-time, life stories of my experiences that connect with scripture and stories from the bible.

The stories in this devotional will help you learn about the Bible's characters and how they relate to our everyday lives. Also, life is tough! Where do we go for help? Who can we share our burdens with? We can share our burdens with God! I'm not sure if you realize that He wants to be ingrained in every part of our lives. God wants to do life with us! "God Thoughts" are just that! His thoughts about our purpose. His thoughts and intentions towards us. His thoughts on the truth about our identity. His thoughts about how we can live a life with Him.

This devotional book is designed to empower you to learn God's word and to learn how God sees you. I want to show you practical ways that God's word can be applied to your daily life through sharing my testimonies to help facilitate personal and spiritual growth. As you read each topic, it will help you set aside time weekly to study, learn how to cultivate a relationship with God, and learn how to adopt His thoughts on how we should live our lives. Know that you are not alone as you navigate different seasons of life. I want to encourage you to know that you have a God who wants to help you.

Thought-provoking questions are provided at the end of each topic to help you ponder and self-reflect on how to address current life circumstances.

Destiny Green

God's Thoughts

God's thoughts about human beings are unimaginable. It's hard for us to wrap our heads around His love for us and the thoughts that He thinks of us. If a person wants to know how God feels about them, they will find it in the Bible. As you read through each page, you will see that God's intended purpose is for you to be like Him. To create, to rule over, to take  care of, to depend on Him (Genesis 1). You will read the promises He makes to those who put their trust in Him. He will care for, protect, give wisdom, walk them to the truth of who He is, and lead them to their purpose. God will teach us how to fight in faith and fight in love. God allows us to express our emotions and tell Him about all our fears. Moses told God that he was not worthy to lead His people. He told God about his speech impediment, and what did God do? He reassured him that he would be able to. Gideon felt the same; he didn't feel worthy to lead the Israelites against the Midianites to victory. Gideon responded to the Lord, telling Him his family was poor and that he was the least one to be chosen in his family to lead the people. God's thoughts were to encourage him and call him a mighty man of valor. David was a man who committed murder intentionally, but he accepted his mistake and knew that he would suffer the consequences. David still chose to serve God, and the words God spoke about him was that he was a man after God's heart. King Nebuchadnezzar was an influential king who reigned for a long time, but his pride ended up bringing him down. Though he had to pay the consequences of his pride for seven years, the Lord thought enough of King Nebuchadnezzar to give him another chance, and he was restored to reign on his throne again. From that moment, King Nebuchadnezzar knew and served the God of Israel (Daniel 4). God's thoughts about the woman who was caught in adultery: When the accusers wanted to punish her, the Lord told them to cast the first stone only if they didn't have any sin. No one could throw a stone at the woman because they also had sinned like her. God spoke to her and told her He wouldn't condemn her and encouraged her not to sin anymore. When the Lord spoke to the woman at the well, He told her about her not being married, and she realized who she was talking to when He offered her to drink the water He had so she wouldn't thirst again. In all these encounters with God, He never condemned these men and women; He showed them mercy, gave them power, delivered them, and healed them. He restored their lives and showed them the life He intended for them and His chosen people. He showed them they were useful with their flaws as long as they were dependent upon Him. Isaiah 55:8 says that God's thoughts and our thoughts are not the same. His thoughts towards us are for peace, full of love, and full of greatness (Jeremiah 29:11). God calls us strong and courageous. He calls us fearfully and wonderfully made, meaning He put a lot of thought and intention into forming us. God's thoughts about us are intentional, and they are not last minute like man's.

Questions/Thoughts:

1. What thoughts do you have about yourself?
2. Are your thoughts in line with what God thinks about you? If not, you can change your thinking today by reading and declaring what the word says.

NOTES:

_____

_____

_____

_____

_____

_____

_____

_____

Vision

Vision is important for everyone to have. Vision is the ability to think about or plan the future with imagination or wisdom.[1] There is a what, why, and how to vision. What are you going to do? How are you going to do it? Why are you doing it? In order to know where you are going, you have to know where you came from, where you are now, and a plan on how to get there. A dream can be considered a vision because people imagine themselves in a specific place doing specific things. As a child, I was asked, what do I want to be when I grow up? I used to say a teacher or a nurse. I knew that I wanted to help people. I just didn't know what that really looked like. As I started getting older and seeking out my purpose, I started to look at my gifts and talents, things that came naturally to me or that brought me joy. Society teaches us that we seek out purpose through vocation. This entails working different jobs, volunteering, and going to school or college. This is how I was able to find what I liked to do and what I didn't like to do. This is how I was able to find out my strengths and weaknesses. Now, I want to take this word vision a step further. I want to inform you that God has a vision for creation. God's vision for creation is found in Genesis 1:26-30. We were created in his likeness and image, and He has called us to rule over and multiply on earth. God gave us dominion, his power, and authority to rule the earth. Well, in order to do so, we have to know our gifts, talents, and abilities. As we learn and continue to practice our gifts, talents, and abilities, we become stronger and more confident in them. Not only that, God will multiply what we have (Matthew 25:14-30). Our gifts come from God for his vision to be carried out on the earth (James 1:17, Ephesians 2:10, 1 Peter 4:10). You may be a person who is saying yes, I know these things about vision. What about when you are waiting for what you thought would have happened by now, and nothing is happening? I have a scripture for that as well: Habakkuk 2:2-3. The passage tells us that though we have been waiting a long time, it will come to pass and not be delayed. The important things to talk about while waiting on vision are: what are you

---

[1] vision, v. meanings, etymology and more | Oxford English Dictionary (oed.com)

doing while you wait? Who are you while you're waiting for the vision to be fulfilled? This is the first question. Are you growing in your gifts, talents, and abilities? For example, If you are a person in leadership, you usually start with the small jobs before doing the big jobs. In order to manage people, you should be a person that is desirable to manage. Be on time, perform assigned tasks, take breaks when scheduled, do not take company products, or be on the phone or computer when it's not your break. Why is this important? When you become a leader, you have to manage people on your team who will perform the same duties as you are performing a higher set of duties. This runs into the second question: what type of person are you while you're waiting? Being trustworthy, honest, fair, dependable, easy to work with, etc. All these qualities matter. Character matters, and it is important to God. It sets the precedence on how you will be blessed and the responsibility God will give us when we display his character or attributes (Galatians 5:22-23). The person who was given more talents was a person who did not quit, a person who was resilient under pressure, a person who didn't allow circumstances or people to stop their drive, and a person who knew the bigger picture of the assignment. I believe this is key to the vision coming to pass. An important thing to remember about waiting on the vision is that we are not responsible for bringing it to pass. That's God's responsibility. We are to tarry with it. Stay in our places and occupy the divine spaces until God tells us to change places or spaces. Tarry also means to linger. Things happen to us and for us, as we wait and linger for the vision to come to pass.

Questions/Thoughts:

1. Does your vision line up with God's purpose for you? If not, what are the steps you need to take to be aligned with God's will for your life? Please answer the questions in the passage and reflect on your responses.

NOTES:

God Is Concerned About The Things You Are Concerned About

Do you know that God is concerned about the things you are concerned about? I want to remind you that He is! Whatever the circumstance or issue, God is concerned about it, and He has a solution for it. All your personal issues, insecurities, flaws, and all the issues of the world, God is concerned about. God knows your family, children, job, career, relationships, health, financial wealth, and children's future are important to you. All of those things are important to Him as well. Psalms 138:8 says, "The Lord will perfect that which concerns me." Whatever that is to you, He wants to perfect it. Concern means a matter of importance to someone.[2] We are important to God, and He has already ordered a path we should walk in; we just have to discover what that is. Philippians 4:6-7 tells us, "Be anxious for nothing, but in everything by prayer and supplication, with thanksgiving, let your requests be made known to God and the peace of God, which surpasses all understanding, will guard your hearts and minds through Christ Jesus." 1 Peter 5:7 says, "Casting all your care upon Him; for He cares for you." I know it can be hard to wrap our minds around this truth because we view God from the lens of our relationships with people, and our experiences have shown that people are not reliable, but God is not like man. He is reliable. We must trust him. God is not a man, that He should lie; neither the son of man, that He should repent: has He said, and shall He not do it? Or has He spoken, and shall He not make it good? (Numbers 23:19 KJV) Let's practice giving God our concerns. First, I want you to think about every concern you have and write it down on paper. Second, find a scripture and speak over every concern. Next, take every concern to God and pray about those concerns. Lastly, wait for God to give you direction, instruction, wisdom, and guidance regarding what He needs you to do next. Some of the answers to our concerns will come from our participation. The other answers will come from God orchestrating the outcome.

---

[2] concern, v. meanings, etymology and more | Oxford English Dictionary. (n.d.). https://www.oed.com/dictionary/concern_v?tl=true

Now, watch how God begins to move in your life and family. I would like to share with you some real-life concerns I had and how God heard me and answered them. I have an African American son that I was worried about raising in this world. I had to have police talks with him, which is what he should do if he is stopped by them, and many talks about the company he needs to keep so he doesn't get caught up in any injustice. I asked the Lord not to allow me to have to visit him in jail or bury him due to premature death. I prayed all the time, and the Lord told me one day when I was washing dishes in my kitchen that I would not experience this as a parent. I believed what He said to me but still worried as a parent at times. That concern doesn't haunt me anymore, though I know anything can still happen. My son is 31 years old today, and God has kept his promise to me. Another concern I had was when I was living in an apartment complex at two different times in my life. I heard my lady neighbor's being abused. It hurt my heart when I would hear the screams and loud bumping sounds. I feared for their lives. I prayed to the Lord about their situation and spoke life over those women's lives. I bound the spirit of death upon their lives and prayed for justice and mercy concerning their lives. In one instance, the man moved out of the apartment, and in the other instance, the woman moved out of the apartment. God used me to pray in all of these situations and instructed me to access the authority He has given me, which is to declare what I wanted to happen. Though I don't know the outcome of those women's lives now, I believe my prayers saved them from trouble in that season of their lives. I thank God that He came to my rescue and my neighbors' rescue, and guess what? He'll come to yours.

Questions/Thoughts:

1. What things concern you the most? How can you participate in the solution?

NOTES:

I'm Hurting

We all experience pain, and this is something that will never change. What can change is how we handle our pain and our perspective about pain. Usually, we associate pain as a negative. Honestly, who wants to feel pain? I don't think any of us do because it hurts and it's uncomfortable. When I read in the Bible that it pleased the Lord to  bruise his son Jesus (Isaiah 53:10), I was baffled by that statement. I asked the Lord how He could be happy about his son enduring such a horrific death. My mind was only stuck on the pain of what Jesus experienced, as many of us are. When we are dealing with painful situations, we focus on the pain and how it is affecting us instead of what we can experience on the other side once we are healed. When a woman wants to have a baby, she will go through many changes in her body, and she will experience the ultimate pain during labor. Once that baby comes out, the pain subsides tremendously, but she will still feel pain until her body heals. I think this is a good parallel to why the Lord felt pleased that his son would be bruised. He knew that the outcome of this pain was bringing salvation to the world and would give everyone who makes a choice to believe in Christ an opportunity to be a member of the heavenly kingdom. Just as a woman knows that having a baby will cause a lot of pain, she also knows that she will experience joy and love once the baby arrives. The pain will be worth it. The Lord knows that you are hurting and He has a plan for your pain just like He had a plan for Jesus' pain. Now this doesn't mean that all the pain that you have experienced is something that He wanted to happen to you, but He will make that pain that you have experienced or are experiencing work out for your good (Romans 8:28). He has done it throughout the Bible for the leaders such as Job, who lost all his livestock, all his children, who was stricken with a disease but God healed him and gave him back double for all that was lost and restored his health (Job 42). He did it for Paul and Silas too. They were beaten for the sake of spreading the gospel, but God delivered them from the enemy every time (Act 16). David is another person who endured the pain of the king he admired trying to kill him because he became jealous of him. God allowed him to escape his plots every time and helped him to continue to honor him as king (1 Samuel 19:9). How hurtful is that to be good to the person who is purposely doing things to hurt you and hinder you? Learn to deal with pain differently. Instead of thinking about what pain takes from you, think about what you can learn from your pain and how you can make those bad situations work for you.

Questions/Thoughts:

1. Are you experiencing emotional, physical, or mental pain? The Lord wants to heal you, free you and work a miracle for you. Ask God to reveal to you the purpose for the pain you are experiencing.

NOTES:

_____

_____

_____

_____

_____

_____

_____

_____

_____

_____

_____

Will You Give God The Opportunity?

"Opportunity" is a word that we all want to experience in our everyday lives. Opportunity means a chance for success or advancement.[3] Sign me up for that, please! Everyone in life gets an opportunity to succeed or advance. No one is left out of this equation. Have you ever heard the saying when opportunity knocks, open the door? Well, this is true, and  the Bible tells us in Ecclesiastes 9:11 that time and chance happen to us all. That simply means that everyone gets an opportunity. I want you to know that God wants to give you an opportunity to have an abundant life. That means plentiful. He wants us to have plenty in our lives for ourselves, our family, neighbors and communities. Some synonyms of opportunity are "opening", "break", or "shot". The word "opportunity" is the root word that comes from the Latin phrase *ob portum veniens*, which means "coming toward port".[4] This also refers to a favorable wind blowing ships into the harbor. So when God gives you an opportunity, He is blowing the ship your way. Can you imagine being lost at sea due to a storm that blew your boat in another direction, and another ship is on the sea looking for you? Can you imagine seeing that ship coming your way and the excitement you'd have about not being forgotten and being rescued? This is what God does for us. He will cause his winds to blow on the circumstances in our life and create opportunities of rescue, provision and purpose for his children. He did it for Noah, when He promised to use him to repopulate the earth and save his family, as stated in Genesis 8:1 (NLT): "But God remembered Noah and all the wild animals and livestock with him in the boat. He sent a wind to blow across the earth, and the floodwaters began to recede." He did it for Moses when He rescued him and the Israelites from their enemies in Exodus 14:21 (NLT): "Then Moses raised his hand over the sea, and the Lord opened up a path through the water with a strong east wind. The wind blew all that night, turning the seabed into dry land." He did it for the Israelites when He promised to feed them daily while they were in the wilderness,

---

[3] Dictionary.com | Meanings & Definitions of English Words. (2021). In Dictionary.com. https://www.dictionary.com/browse/opportunity
[4] Vocabulary.com. (n.d.). Opportunity. In Vocabulary.com Dictionary. Retrieved from https://www.vocabulary.com/dictionary/opportunity

as described in Numbers 11:31: "Now the Lord sent a wind that brought quail from the sea and let them fall all around the camp. For miles in every direction there were quail flying about three feet above the ground." Lastly, He caused a wind to blow Jonah's way when he was being disobedient to his assignment and was trying to hide from God. Jonah 1:4 mentions the event as: "But the Lord hurled a powerful wind over the sea, causing a violent storm that threatened to break the ship apart." So, whether you are hiding from God, whether you need God to provide your daily needs, whether you are facing opposition in life, or whether God performs a miracle to keep his promises to you, know that God can cause the winds to blow in your life that can create opportunities to work in your favor!

Questions/Thoughts:

1. What winds have blown in your life? Are they warning signs from God that you have left your assignment or signs that God is providing for you in this season?

NOTES:

_____

_____

_____

_____

_____

_____

_____

Enjoying Your Life

Enjoying our lives is difficult for most of us because we allow the outside circumstances to dictate how we feel. We even let things we desire or just simply want that haven't happened yet, and don't have yet, to predict our attitude and the way we enjoy our lives. What if I told you we don't have to do that? What if I told you we can make a choice to enjoy our lives every day even if it's the toughest season of our lives? This is something that I am learning to do, and the phrase 'I am', is present tense, because I have to constantly make a daily choice to choose to enjoy my life, no matter what the circumstances are in my life. The Lord spoke so clearly to me recently, that one of the reasons we can enjoy our lives, in spite of what is happening around us and in our situations, is because seasons change. Whew! I truly thank God for this! Ecclesiastes 3 clearly tells us about all the seasons we will experience in life. Some of us may experience them at the same time and others at different times in our lives, but nonetheless, the season will change! This lets us know a few things: one, we have no control over the seasons we will face, but we do have control on how to respond during these seasons. Second, since going through these seasons of life is a principle (won't change), I have a choice in how I'm going to approach these seasons. And by this, I mean I get to choose my attitude, my mood, and what I speak out of my mouth during these seasons. I get to choose how I will fight in these seasons. 1 Peter 4:12 (NCV) says, "My friends, do not be surprised at the terrible trouble which now comes to test you. Do not think that something strange is happening to you." This scripture has become one of my favorites because it reminds me not to go down the rabbit hole in my mindset, feelings, and emotions about people or God when I am experiencing a season I don't want to be in. Who wants to be in a time of war, a time of tearing down, a time of hate, a time of refraining from embracing, a time of crying, a time of throwing away things, and a time of being sad? Especially if we have made poor choices, which we all do. But the flip side is, we will experience peace, building up, love, embracing, laughter, keeping things, joy, and sowing. Job 2:10 mentions the question Job asked his wife, "Should we accept only good things from God and not trouble?" To be honest, those who haven't learned to navigate through life's seasons and allow depression, anxiety, and worry to take over their mindsets, attitudes, feelings, and emotions are people who have not matured in their faith (1 Corinthians 14:20, 1 Corinthians 3:1-3, Romans 12:2, Luke 8:14). They are people who don't know what God says about them and their situation. They don't know the access they have in the Kingdom to exercise their authority over their circumstances, emotions, feelings, attitudes, and mindsets (2 Corinthians 10:3-5). They don't know the investment God made in His creation and how He wants them to belong (John 3:16). It's safe to say that we all forget about His promises that are yes and amen (2 Corinthians 1:20). My prayer for those of you reading this is that you will have a change of heart about how you view the difficult seasons and circumstances you face in your life. You don't need what you think you need to enjoy your life every day when you belong to the Creator. Your circumstances make you a conduit, a vessel for the Master's use, to share your hope, testimony, and faith to help others in the body of Christ (2 Corinthians 1:3-4, 1 Peter 1:6-7).

Questions/Thoughts:

1. Have you maximized the opportunities to enjoy your life daily no matter the season of life you are in? If so How? If not, what steps can you take to change this?

NOTES:

_____

_____

_____

_____

_____

Eight Dimensions to Wellness

Do you know that there are eight dimensions to our wellness? It's just like having eight pieces of a whole pie. Have you ever heard someone say, "I want the whole pie?" This is what they were referring to: wholeness. If you don't know what the eight dimensions are, I would like to share them with you. According to Dr Peggy Swarbrick and Jay  Yudof, we have emotional health, environmental health, financial health, intellectual health, occupational health, physical health, social health, and spiritual health. How are you coping with life? Does your environment support the type of person you want to be and what you want out of life? How is your financial status? Do you have enough living expenses for you and your family? Are your assets protected? What type of information are you feeding your mind? Are you satisfied with the type of work you currently do? What state is your physical health in? Can you assess your relationships and determine if they are healthy and if they support where you are going in life? Lastly, how do you nurture your spiritual health? All of these aspects are imperative for growth and purpose. There should be continuous growth in all of these aspects of our lives, just as there are life stages in our growth and development. There are stages to our growth and development in the aspects of wellness. We have the power to reach the highest level of success in our lives. We get to make choices about what we want or don't want in our lives, or who we want and don't want in our lives. God loves us so much that He gave us the power to choose (Genesis 2:16 and 2:20). Although we don't have control over how the seasons of life may change and most times don't have any control over the different life experiences we may face, we can rest assured in what God has promised us: to be with us (Matthew 28:20), to give us wisdom (James 1:5), and to make all grace abound toward us so that we have everything we need (2 Corinthians 9:8). It's time to take an assessment of your life today and locate where you are so you can make a plan to move to a different location. A place where you have fulfillment. A place you are dominating. Our circumstances should not have dominion over us. We are created to have dominion over our circumstances. We have the power to speak how our circumstances should work for us. If you are finding yourself in a place of lack, you have the ability to speak that lack will not live in your space and make the necessary decisions and adjustments to move out of that place. I want to ask you the same question that Jesus asked the man at the pool. Do you want to be well?[5] (John 5:6)

Questions/Thoughts:

1. What can you do today to grow in these aspects of wellness?

NOTES:

_____

_____

_____

_____

_____

_____

_____

_____

_____

_____

_____

---

[5] https://www.center4healthandsdc.org/uploads/7/1/1/4/71142589/wellness_in_8_dimensions_booklet_with_daily_plan.pdf

God's Faithfulness

The word "faithful" means to remain loyal and steadfast.[6] Do you have any experiences in your relationships of any kind where someone was loyal to you and steady in that relationship? If you do, you should count your blessings. It is hard to find friendships, romantic relationships, and business relationships where people experience consistency and loyalty  throughout the duration of those relationships without ill motives or some type of betrayal occurring. We don't have to worry about this with God. The scripture says that He is faithful and true (Revelation 19:11), and He has proven this to us time and time again. God created a rainbow as a sign of His covenant that He wouldn't flood the whole earth to wipe out mankind again (Genesis 9:13). To this day, we still see a rainbow after it rains, and it makes me smile. When the Israelites were in the wilderness for 40 years, God provided their daily food, manna from heaven, or quail when they complained about wanting meat to eat (Exodus 16:4). When Paul and Silas were thrown in prison for casting out demons, they were bound and shackled, but as they began to sing praises to the Lord at midnight, they were freed (Acts 16:25-34). Daniel was thrown into the lion's den because he would not bow down to the king and his ways of doing things, but the Lord provided safety in that den by closing the mouths of the lions (Daniel 6:22). God allowed Nehemiah to rebuild the wall of Jerusalem and protected him from the schemes of Sanballat and Tobiah, as they were trying to stop the work (Nehemiah 6). Jesus was betrayed by Judas, one of His disciples whom He had chosen to demonstrate and preach what the kingdom is all about. Jesus did not let the betrayal of Judas hinder His purpose to die for the world so He could save the world by His sacrifice. Here are a few stories of God's faithfulness to me: He delivered me from a pit of depression, providing a community around me to support me when I didn't have my family around. I remember one summer month when I lived in Iowa, I turned off my gas to save money. On a particularly cool night, which made it cool inside my home, I decided to bring my gas grill into the house for a heat source. Just

---

[6] faithful, adj., n., & adv. meanings, etymology and more | Oxford English Dictionary. (n.d.). https://www.oed.com/dictionary/faithful_adj?tab=meaning_and_use

as I was about to light it up, the doorbell rang. When I went to the door, I didn't see anyone. So, I walked onto my porch, looking around, and then looked in my mailbox. There were 14 child support checks in the mailbox. I started shouting and crying!

There are so many other stories about God's faithfulness to a world that wasn't and still isn't faithful to Him, yet He still died a tragic death so that we could have a chance at life. What is your story about God's faithfulness to you? Did He heal you from a disease? Did He save you from an accident? Did He deliver you from an addiction? Whatever it is, just know He showed His loyalty to you by providing what you needed. God was consistent in His love, mercy, and kindness towards you. He doesn't hold out on His mercy, grace, and favor when we don't do what He requires of us; this is what makes Him different from mankind. It's not in His nature to withhold (Psalm 84:11). It is in His nature to give.

Questions/Thoughts:

1. How can you show your loyalty and consistency in your relationship to God?

NOTES:

_____

_____

_____

_____

_____

_____

_____

He Lifted My Bowed Down Head

There is a saying people often use: "walk with your head held high," which simply means to walk confidently and proudly. When someone walks with their head bowed down, it usually signifies defeat, sadness, or hopelessness. I don't know how many times I've had to tell my children, or other children I've seen walking with their heads down, to  walk with their heads up. I tell them this not only to encourage them but also to let them know that you can't see where you're going when your head is down. It is dangerous for anyone to walk with their head down. The word "bowed" means bent downward and forward. Some synonyms for bowed are declining, weeping, hanging, and drooping.[7] King David makes many references in the book of Psalms to having a bowed head and God being the lifter of his head. Due to David's sin of murdering an innocent man for his selfish gain, he had to face the consequences (2 Samuel 12). David was forgiven by God and was repentant for what he had done. He understood his actions and the consequences, and he held on to his hope in God for victory. We all have made poor, selfish choices like David and have had to pay, or are paying, the consequences of those choices. For others, life just happens, causing sadness, grief, despair, and hopelessness, but we can rest assured in the hope we have in God that He will see us through. Psalm 3:3 says, "But you, O LORD, are a shield around me; you are my glory, the one who holds my head high." In Psalm 42:5, the author asks, "Why am I discouraged? Why is my heart so sad? I will put my hope in God! I will praise Him again—my Savior and my God!" I remember my head being bowed down when I had to leave the first church I grew up in due to inappropriate actions by the pastor who filled in. I remember being hurt and angry that the pastor was not held accountable for his actions. I was confused about whether I did the right thing by speaking up and felt lost because that church was all I knew for 16 years of my life. Later in life, I understood that situation was a crossroad in my life to go to another level in my relationship with God and learn how to have a relationship with God whom I was

---

[7] Merriam-Webster. (n.d.). Bowing. In Merriam-Webster.com thesaurus. Retrieved from https://www.merriam-webster.com/thesaurus/bowing

introduced to and believed in as a child. God has healed me of my pain from that situation, and I am able to sympathize and have compassion for others who have had similar experiences. I can tell them that God lifted my bowed head. He wiped away every tear I cried and gave me joy. Whatever the reason your head is hanging or drooping low, whatever is causing your hope to decline, I want you to know that God wants to lift you up. He wants to bring you out of a horrible pit, out of the miry clay, and set your feet upon a rock, establishing your steps (Psalm 40:2).

Questions/Thoughts:

1. What are you sad about today? What or who is causing your hope to decline? Do you believe God can change you and your situation now?

NOTES:

_____

_____

_____

_____

_____

_____

_____

_____

_____

_____

Keep Your Word To Yourself

This is the phrase that will ring loud in my ears as I pursue my goals in life: "When I tell someone I'm going to do something for them, I make sure to follow through." Why? Because I want others to know that I'm dependable, trustworthy, and accountable. I take pride in following through if I volunteer or give someone my word that I will do something. I do this because I don't want anyone flaking on me. If someone tells me they are going to do something for me or be a part of something, I count them in, and if they don't show up, I expect that an emergency happened as to why they couldn't show up. If not, I make a mental note that I can't depend on them. One of my struggles is inconsistency. I once navigated a season in my life where I was a single parent, went back to college, was in a failing marriage, all while having to still work, be a leader in the church, and complete internships. When I think about this, it amazes me how I was able to conquer this season of my life because there were twists and turns along the way. In spite of the unexpected, I was able to stay focused and keep my eye on the end goal. On the other hand, I can set a goal about cutting certain things out of my diet or start a project of some sort and not see it through to completion. That frustrates me so much! I would always pray to God about this, asking Him to help me with this flaw. As I was preparing for the new year 2023, God spoke to me and said, "Keep your word to yourself." I jumped out of my bed when I heard this because it became clear as day why I had been wrestling with inconsistency. The same energy I had for going to school and all the other responsibilities I had, no matter what popped up that tried to distract me, or situations I had to deal with, I didn't let that stop my focus. Do you know how important you are? Do you know that the focus and determination you had in one season can transfer to a different season in your life, bigger and better? If you can keep your word to others, then you can keep your word to yourself. The same reason you feel about keeping your word to others is the same reason you should feel about keeping your word to yourself. Keep your word to yourself because you don't want to let yourself down. You don't want to feel bad about yourself. You don't want to abandon your assignment. The scripture says, "Let your yes be yes, and your no, no; anything beyond this comes from the evil one" (Matthew 5:37). You can't expect God to bless your plan if you are indecisive. You can't see a goal to its completion if you waver back and forth with starting and stopping. Once you start, don't stop until it's accomplished!

Questions/Thoughts:

1. Do you struggle with keeping your word to yourself? Why is this an issue for you? Assess your motives for specific goals you set! Submit your plans to God and ask Him to give you direction and to make sure they are in line with his will.

NOTES:

_____
_____
_____
_____
_____
_____
_____
_____
_____
_____

Vices That Hinder Purpose

"Vice" is a word that I haven't heard often, but it is parallel to the scripture that says, "It's the little foxes that spoil the vine" (Song of Solomon 2:15). The Bible warns us about what these little foxes are: jealousy, hatred, covetousness, gossip, lying, stealing, unforgiveness, bitterness, complaining. According to Wikipedia, a vice can refer to a  fault, a negative character trait, a defect, an infirmity, or a bad or unhealthy habit.[8] All these vices mentioned can hinder our purpose. You must know that purpose is not one specific thing; it's our journey to what God has for us. These vices can destroy our character. These vices can destroy relationships. The Bible says that He is the vine and we are the branches. We need to be connected to the vine in order to thrive in our purpose. We get our nutrients from the vine. If we practice these vices more often than not, we will be cut off from the vine because the fruit these vices produce is opposite of what God wants to see in us and in our lives (John 15:1-8). Our life should be a mirror of God's character and power. The scripture says that we are made in His image and these vices mentioned are not His character; they are the character of the devil, the one who comes to steal, kill, and destroy. We don't have to be jealous or covet another's life because God has a plan and purpose for everyone's life that He designed (Jeremiah 29:11). God is a wonderful creator, by the way. The clouds in the sky, the air you can't see, the grass that grows in the season it's designed to grow in—Genesis 1. That is all God. I want to encourage you not to allow these vices to hinder the plans and purposes of God. We have the power to live the way we want. I know there are horrible circumstances in the world that affect our lives and the way we live them, such as water crises, severe poverty in third-world countries, homelessness, and war-stricken countries, but we can take God at His word and watch Him perform it! Somehow and someway, He will! God is not surprised by all that is going on in the world, and He has a solution for it. We can be part of the solution if we don't allow these vices to latch onto our character and live them out in our lives. I want to share a

---

[8] Wikipedia contributors. (2024, June 19). Vice. In Wikipedia, The Free Encyclopedia. Retrieved from https://en.wikipedia.org/w/index.php?title=Vice&oldid=1229943067

story from the Bible about Joseph. He was sent to prison based on a lie told by his superior's wife. She lusted after him and wanted to sleep with him, but he turned her down. When he ran out of her presence, resisting her advances, she reached out for him and took a piece of his clothes. She knew how much her husband admired and trusted Joseph. So, she made up a lie about him trying to rape her. Joseph ended up being thrown into prison and he was there a long time. He thought God had forgotten about him, but in the midst of being in prison, God favored him. Joseph also experienced jealousy from his brothers who tried to kill him, but he forgave his brothers and ended up providing for his entire family in the midst of a seven-year famine (Genesis 39 and 37). So, the wife's lust and lies (vices) caused an innocent man to be imprisoned. Take an assessment of your heart and ask God to deliver you and heal you from these little foxes."

Questions/Thoughts:

1. What character traits or unhealthy habits do you need God to deliver you from? How have these vices hindered your life? Have your vices caused trouble in others' lives? If so, how can you correct this?

NOTES:

_____

_____

_____

_____

_____

_____

Do you have Unforgiveness Lingering in your Heart?

Forgiveness is not an easy road to travel on because the majority of us feel justified in our hearts on why we decide not to forgive those who have caused us pain, hurt, and difficulty in our lives. The truth is, we all need forgiveness, and because we do, we must give it to receive it. Matthew 6:14 says, "For if you forgive other people when they sin against you, your heavenly Father will also forgive you." Luke 6:37 says, "Forgive, and you will be forgiven." God has given us some principles to live by, and this is one of them. Our minds are not like God's. When we think about forgiving someone for doing something wrong to us, we think we are giving them a pass. The truth is we cannot control anyone but ourselves. So if a person has ill motives, it may be true that they think they can continue to treat you wrong. We can't change that, only God can. I know there are many horrible experiences people endure. I don't want to minimize your pain; it's valid. I just want you to know that you can get to a place where you can forgive. Job's wife told him to curse his God and die because she couldn't understand why he would want to serve a God that took everything from him, all his children, all his livestock, and cursed him with a disease. The scripture tells us that Job was a righteous man, but he faced great difficulty where he started to question God about what he was experiencing. He was trying to make sense of it (Job 7). Saul turned on David because he became jealous of his anointing and power. Saul hunted him down to kill him, but David forgave him, and when he had a chance to kill Saul, he didn't, because he respected him as the king (1 Samuel 24:6). Finally, Jesus was wrongly persecuted by His people. The King knew He wasn't a criminal and had nothing on Him. His people didn't understand why He called Himself God because He didn't look like what they expected from a king (Matthew 27). So, Jesus was beaten all the way to the cross and gave up His life for the world. Why? Because the world was in sin, and He had to be the sacrifice for our souls to be saved. I don't know how people can be so evil and cause such pain to others that it basically ruins lives because many never recover, but I do know that God will rescue us from all of our troubles and He will heal all of our diseases. I also know that we have caused someone hurt and pain, and if not to others, to God, and we all need His forgiveness. I just want to encourage you to open up your heart to allow God into those unforgiven lingering places. This is one of the things you don't have to feel good about doing; you just have to do it because it pleases God and it's the right thing to do. I personally still need help with certain people because when I hear their names, I remember those experiences. But the good news is I also remember how far God has brought me in my healing process and how I didn't let those moments define me. I found purpose! I have joy because I was able to let those emotions go. Guess what? When those emotions want to come visit me, I don't open the door!

Questions/Thoughts:

1. Who do you need to forgive? What emotions are still lingering in your heart from those painful experiences? Have you given it to God? Do you want to be free from those emotions? You don't have to understand why things happened the way they did to be healed from it.

NOTES:

_____
_____
_____
_____
_____
_____
_____

Loving Others That Have Wronged You

I know it is not easy to love others that have wronged you but we have to learn how to do this. The scripture tells us it's easy to love those that love us back but we have to love others that steal from us. We have to love others that purposely talk about us and slander our names. We have to love those that mistreat us and this is the difficult part (Luke 6: 27-  36). For me, if a person that I don't have to deal with in my everyday life mistreats me; I can get over that because I have no connection to them. If the person I have to forgive is a family member, my children or a spouse, that's when it becomes difficult because I can't just get rid of them. I have to learn how to build a relationship with them through the conflict. Conflict is normal in relationships because people have emotions and experiences. Depending on those experiences and how people were treated will be the catalyst on how they will treat others in relationships. I remember reading my word in a season of my life when I was really broken and full of hurt. The Lord had me read 1 Corinthians 13, and I would become so furious while reading this chapter because I was so angry with my child's father. I had gone through some very traumatic situations with him and I had to deal with him because I wanted my daughter to have a relationship with him. The relationship between him and I was toxic to say the least. I really tried to do and say the right things but it was very difficult for me. I felt taunted and manipulated by him in this relationship which made it very difficult for me to deal with him. So, in reading this particular chapter, every time I would read love is patient, love is kind, love doesn't dishonor, love keeps no record of wrong. I would cringe! It was like someone writing with chalk on the chalkboard making that screeching sound. I would become so frustrated that I would throw my Bible across the room because I couldn't bear the thought of showing love to this person that is purposely mistreating me. I was mad at God that He was allowing this to happen to me because I didn't deserve this. Now first, you may be thinking you threw your Bible across the room? That is blasphemy! But no! This was a real moment and I want to let you know that God is not surprised by anyone's reaction on how they may respond to seeking to obey his word. That was my flesh that was screeching. My spirit wanted to do what was right; otherwise, I would not have sought God (Matthew 26:41). This may be you screeching at the thought of having to love those that are hurting or have hurt you. I want to let you know that you can do it. That season of my life has long passed and I had a lot of falls during that season but I got back up to try again every time. To make loving more practical, it's just taking the opportunity to do or say the right thing vs doing or saying the wrong thing, and when difficult people have to be a part of our lives we have lots of opportunities to practice. One of the ways that will help you get to this place to love is allowing God to heal your heart from those horrible experiences. The Lord made a promise in his word that He will deliver us from our distress, so let Him do it (Psalms 107:6)!

Questions/Thoughts:

1. Which person are you finding difficult to love right now? Some things that will help you through this process is not talking bad or negative about them. Pray about the situation and read scriptures for God to heal your heart. Let God avenge the situation because He can do a better job than we can.

NOTES:

_____

_____

_____

_____

_____

_____

Judging Others

If we could get a dollar for every time we have judged someone out of our mouths we would be rich. This tongue is hard to tame and the scripture tells us it can start a fire. The tongue is a rudder that steers conversations (James 3:5). It is easy to say what you will or won't do in a situation that you are not in. Why? Because you are not in it. People  wonder how someone can steal, rob, cheat, or kill. The bottom line is the majority of people do not set their day to do these things. There are a combination of circumstances that take place before these things just happen. I'm a social worker and one of the things I love about social work is we look at the entire life of a person on how they ended up in their situation. If a person is living in poverty, homeless or in an abusive situation, we take the time out to seek out what landed them in this place and problem solve solutions to get them out or to help them maintain from there. You always hear people say about homeless people, "just get a job", or a person that has mental health issues, "just take your medication" or "just see a psychiatrist", and it is not as easy as 1, 2, 3! The fact is people's problems are more complicated than what meets the eye and we have to learn how to be merciful in our speech (Matthew 5:7). The scripture tells us when we judge others the same measure we used will be given back to us. Meaning, you are going to experience a situation like the one you're judging and then we'll see what you're gonna do. 9 out of 10 times, you're gonna do what you said you wouldn't do and you are going to want mercy and understanding (Matthew 7:1-5). I remember saying I would not tolerate a cheating husband, but I did. When I harshly judged others that would take back their cheating spouses; I said words like, "they are stupid", "I would never deal with that", "if my husband cheats on me that is it!" "I'm ending my marriage!" Well, when my husband cheated on me, I didn't end my marriage right away, I chose to work through my marriage. I felt stupid and remembered those words that I spoke out of my mouth against others. I remember another time speaking against a male cousin that went to prison. I judged the parents of not being spiritual enough and praying to God about their child and thought they must have not instilled in him God's word because that wouldn't have happened. How naive and immature I was. I was a young Christian and at that stage in my life, I was very critical with my speech and judgmental towards others. I thought by being saved and pursuing God, I would escape all those types of situations. I was raising two children and as my children became older they did things they knew better not to do. So, the moral of this story is no matter how I taught my children about God, they will still do things against His will and it didn't mean that I was a bad or neglectful parent. Now in my life, I'm learning to bridle my tongue. I'm learning to be gracious with my speech because I want to receive that same measure.

Questions /Thoughts:

1. Whom have you judged? Can you remember a time that you received the same measure of what you have spoken? Ask God for forgiveness and the people you have judged if you can, for forgiveness so that you can receive mercy. Let's learn to think before we speak. This will be beneficial for everyone around us!

NOTES:

_____

_____

_____

_____

_____

_____

_____

Pray For The Women and Children

The more I navigate in this life as a woman, the more I'm understanding why God said to pray for the women and children (Luke 23:28). Though the Lord said this in regards to the suffering that was about to take place on his people from the Romans, this type of suffering is still happening today. Abortions, rapes, exploitations of all kinds, abuse and neglect are situations the world continues to address. The statistics are high when it comes to single parent households. These households usually are women that are taking care of their children. Women endure so much! Abuse, rape, racism, sexism, ageism, prejudices. Gender inequality is real! The world is still fighting for women to make equal pay to what men make while doing the same jobs. Around the world, 104 countries have gender discrimination encoded in laws about employment.[9] I read in an article from World Vision, women are still fighting to be heard and seen.[10] Women are the greatest number of the population living in poverty with their children. In another article, Adoption.com posted in 2019 says, "Worldwide, an estimated 300 million children are subjected to violence, exploitation, and abuse. Practices include the worst forms of child labor, armed conflict, and harmful practices such as female genital mutilation, cutting and child marriage."[11] We all have heard the saying that children are our future and they are! Since this is true, what does this mean if our children are experiencing these kinds of trauma? That's why God tells us to pray. Then you may ask why would God allow such things like this to happen? My answer is God does not control people and their behaviors. There are so many reasons why people do what they do! It breaks my heart to hear of the horrific experiences women and children face daily but one thing I know for sure is prayer works! Not only praying but getting involved in our communities to be a part and help facilitate change. Through our

---

[9] Women's Workplace Equality Index: Leveling the Playing Field (cfr.org)

[10] Karl, S., Longwe, S., OECD, Dugarova, UN Women, UNDP, & Inter Agency Standing Committee. (2021). CRITICAL PATHWAYS to child well-being: Exploratory research to understand gender equality and women's empowerment pathways and contributions to child well-being. https://www.wvi.org/sites/default/files/2022-04/Womens%20Empowerment%20Literature%20Review_v3.pdf

[11] Global-annual-results-report-2021-goal-area-3.pdf (unicef.org)

prayers, God will raise up people in leadership positions and people with the resources to assist women and children in need of rescue. Just like women nurture and support their children, women need that same support from their families and communities. Women's goals need to be supported. Women need to be validated. Our children need support, guidance and direction. Our children need to know their contribution to the world is important and how to seek that out. We know that blessings and curses are generational. We want the blessings to supersede the curses so we must seek our Father in Heaven and petition for His will to be done on earth as it is in Heaven. We must do our part to create opportunities that will foster love, unity, community and growth (Psalms 133:1-3). That's our responsibility!

Questions /Thoughts:

1. Which women and children do you know that need help? How can you make a difference? If you are a woman, how can you take the necessary steps to heal yourself? If you have children, how can you foster their growth?

NOTES:

_____

_____

_____

_____

_____

_____

_____

Pray For The Women and Children Part 2

In the previous story, I spoke about the significance of women and children, how they are handled in society, and the suffering that women and children endure. I want to speak a little on the significance of women and how women were significant in spreading the gospel of the good news about Jesus. Every encounter that Jesus had with a woman resulted in their lives being immediately impacted and changed. The Samaritan woman at the well (John 4:7-26). The woman who had the issue of bleeding for 12 years (Mark 5:25-34). The woman that washed Jesus' feet; she was considered a sinner, but Jesus did not reject her offering of love (Luke 7:36-50). The women who witnessed Jesus' death, burial, and resurrection, such as Mary Magdalene, Jesus' mother Mary, and Mary, the mother of James and Joseph, just to name a few. These women were significant in spreading the good news that Jesus had risen from the grave and was not at the tomb when they went to visit Him (Luke 24). We can't forget about Eve, the first woman we know that started procreation, which is significant to the purpose of women and the roles they play in our society. There are many women who have played a vital role in my life concerning who I am as a woman. It started with my mother. I am the 5th of six siblings, one is no longer with us. My mother introduced me to God. Going to church was not an option in our home. Her faith in God was the anchor on how we survived and thrived through life's oppositions. Some of the things I learned from my mom are a strong work ethic, taking care of others, having a spirit of generosity, and the most important is being grounded in my faith. I witnessed many of my mom's transitions in life as a woman. She was a divorced, single parent raising 5 of her own children and 3 of her grandchildren, and life was happening, but she stood the test of time. Another woman that played a significant role in my life as a woman is my godmother. She adopted me into her family when I was eleven years old, and I had the opportunity to work with her in ministry for 16 years. What she sowed into me spiritually, I could never repay. I witnessed these two women stare poverty in its face, stare death in its face, stare at the stigma that society places on black women in its face, and they did it with God on their side. God was on the sides of the previous women from the Bible I mentioned earlier. As a result of their faith, my life was impacted and changed. Now, I'm carrying the faith torch to impact others' lives and sharing how I navigated my life experiences through my faith in God. It has been a journey for me learning my significance as a woman, learning my purpose, and accepting who I am and what I am called and chosen to do as a woman. As I stated earlier about stigmas that are placed on women and women of color. Stigmas can stunt the growth of any person if you buy into it. It has stunted the need for unity and growth in our communities. God doesn't disregard women, their importance, or their abilities, and society shouldn't either. I believe it's important to God for society to recognize, support, nurture, and validate women because we are vital to our families and communities.

Questions/Thoughts:

1. Have you bought into any of the stigmas society has placed on women? If so, how can you change this? How can you nurture and support the women around you?

NOTES:

_____

_____

_____

_____

_____

_____

Seasons in Life

Seasons have been established since the foundation of the world in the book of Genesis, and they have been established to sustain themselves. There will always be four seasons on the earth. That will never change (Genesis 8:22). What will change about these seasons is their temperature. This is how we know that a season is ending and a new season is beginning. Though the weather patterns have been off in different parts of the world lately, such as the south experiencing tornadoes, the east experiencing floods and getting slammed with record breaking snowstorms, and the west experiencing record breaking rainfall and mudslides - it is still obvious what seasons we are in. Also, the reason we know the seasons we are in is because the month and day are the indicators of that season. Summer months have been established from June through August. Fall months have been established from September through November. Winter months have been established from December through February and spring months have been established from March through May. This is all God's plan and design for the purpose of life. Life for every creature and human that was created. Life for everything that grows on the earth. Every season has its purpose just as our experiences in life have their purpose. We can call it the seasons of life. Ecclesiastes 3 refers to what they are. I want to take a moment to talk about the temperatures of the seasons. In winter we experience cold, in the spring rain, in the fall cool or mild temperatures and the summer is hot. Now the cold and hot seasons are uncomfortable because what we do is either turn on the heat or air to feel comfortable. The fall temperature is comfortable but the spring temps are somewhat inconvenient. I don't think I know anyone that loves to go out in the rain to run errands, walk in it or travel in it. What do we say when it rains? "Oh, my hair doesn't stand a chance in the rain". "I'm not wearing my new shoes in that wet and muddy mess". "I just washed my car". And it goes on and on. We feel these same emotions in the seasons of life. When things are going well in our lives, prayers are answered, relationships are in a good place, money to pay all the bills, we are satisfied. But the moment we experience the opposite of these situations, we begin to feel uncomfortable and inconvenienced. Well, David said in Psalms, "It was good that I was afflicted that I might learn your statutes". (Psalm 119:71) The seasons of life help us to learn God's ways. The seasons of life help us depend on God like the earth does. The birds depend on God not man. Though man tends to the earth God is the ultimate provider of our earth. The earth is the Lord's, and everything in it, the world, and all who live in it (Psalms 24:1). I just wanted to remind you that seasons are beneficial to our purpose.

Questions/Thoughts:

1. What season of life are you in? How can you adjust your attitude? If you learn how to adjust the temperature of your attitude in the uncomfortable seasons, you'll be able to experience that season with joy and peace.

NOTES:

_____

_____

_____

_____

_____

_____

_____

_____

_____

Defeating Goliaths In Your Life

I want to share with you the story about Goliath and how David was able to defeat him. Goliath was a Philistine who was referred to as a champion, which represented his nation. Goliath and his nation were going to fight against Saul and his nation, Israel. Goliath told Saul, instead of his whole army fighting against the Philistines, he wanted  him to pick one person who represents Israel to fight him, and if he lost, the Philistines would be servants to Israel, but if he won, Israel would be servants to the Philistines. At this point, Saul did not choose anyone to fight against Goliath because he and all the others were afraid of him. Goliath was nine feet tall in stature, and he had some heavy-duty armor that obviously looked intimidating to all who looked upon him. One day, David happened to pay a visit to his brothers to bring them some food and overheard what Goliath was saying to Saul. David also believed Goliath was taunting Saul and his people and thought he wasn't going to take that. David asked Saul what would happen if he fought Goliath and won, and Saul told him the reward he would receive. Though David saw Goliath was huge in stature and had all of this intimidating armor on his body to fight with, David knew he had an advantage over him, and that is, he was circumcised. Circumcision in the Bible meant that God made a covenant with Israel and chose them as His people. David knew that Goliath was not circumcised and knew he had this advantage over him. David knew God would be with him and would help him conquer them as their enemy. Needless to say, David got permission to fight Goliath and killed him. David was not only way smaller than Goliath in stature; he killed him with one stone. David received the rewards for conquering this giant and became the next king in line to the throne (1 Samuel 17). What are you afraid of? Who are you afraid of? I'm here to tell you that you don't have to be afraid of anything or anyone! If you have given your life to God and are part of His family, you have benefits and access to the kingdom, His power, favor, strength, and provision. God is the same yesterday, today, and forevermore. He gave David the courage and power to conquer Goliath, and he was able to do so because he and Israel belonged to God. God has made us promises that we are overcomers. We are more than conquerors. We have everything we need that pertains to life and godliness. Joshua 1:9 says, "Have I not commanded you? Be strong and courageous. Do not be afraid; do not be discouraged, for the LORD your God will be with you wherever you go." Know that you can defeat anything in your life that is bigger and stronger than you; diseases, addictions, breakdowns, breakups, and any fears you have with God on your side. Believers have the same covenant God made with the Israelites. So that's the advantage you have over anything that is bigger and stronger than you!

Questions/Thoughts:

1. Are you saved? If not, if you give your life to Christ right now, He will give you the power to overcome (Romans 10:9-13).

NOTES:

_____

_____

_____

_____

_____

_____

_____

_____

_____

All Things Will Work Together For Your Good

I think this is a promise we all have to be reminded of, especially when we are in the midst of depression, debt, grief, loss of relationships, loss of material things, and just grieving what once was. Know that all of your experiences in life can work out for your good because that's what God promised (Romans 8:28). We can't choose the families we were  born into and the unfortunate circumstances that surround those experiences that have shaped our values and thought processes. One thing we can do is learn the right way of doing things, the right way of living so that we can live fulfilled lives with purpose. Most people can't imagine living a life like this, especially while in the midst of their slimy circumstances, and what I mean by slimy is we can have so many things going on at once that it can cause us to slide into temptation. Take your pick: lying, stealing, cheating, adultery, fornication, having ill motives for others. The slippery slope goes on and on. I've been on the slippery slope, and all I can say is, I was so far, deep in darkness that I could not see my way out! I wanted out and heard that it was possible, but my situation seemed impossible. I'm here to tell you that God pulled me out! Out of depression! Out of low self-esteem! Out of financial ruin! Out of shame! Into a life of purpose and fulfillment. Into a life of peace and joy! Into a life of financial freedom. Into a life of impossible possibilities! He will do the same for you! So, know! All of the closed doors! All of the failed relationships! All of the no's! All of the pain and mistreatment you experience! It will work for your good if you'd allow God's plan! It worked out for Daniel when he was in the lion's den. He decided he would not go down the slippery slope and bow to another god. Because of that decision, God protected him (Daniel 6). It worked out for Job's good. His wife told him to curse the God they both believed in, and he decided to endure the sickness, the loss of his children and livestock, and God gave it all back double, for his faithfulness to Him (Job 1 and 2, Job 42:10). It worked out for Nehemiah. He asked to rebuild the walls of Jerusalem because his heart was in distress over what he once knew was a land that was prosperous and protected, that had now become desolate and torn down. Nehemiah was given permission by the king to rebuild the wall (Nehemiah 2). Guess what? You have been given permission to rebuild your walls. You have God's permission to rebuild your joy, peace, family, finances, and your future now! You no longer have to grieve what once was. God will cause all things to work together for your good now! So let Him work it.

Questions/Thoughts:

1. Do you believe that your experiences can work for your purpose? What are the walls in your life that have brought you distress? What are the walls in your life that need to be rebuilt?

NOTES:

_____

_____

_____

_____

_____

_____

_____

_____

_____

_____

_____

Get Busy

These two words really don't need an explanation. When I was a child, my mom told me to get busy, or the teacher at school told me to get busy. I knew exactly what that meant. The reason why they would tell us to get busy was because they knew we were given an assignment and they observed us being distracted by something or someone. Our parents and teachers not only knew we were distracted by someone or something but they also knew we were bothered by something through observing our dismissive behaviors and attitudes. In order for a student to be given homework, the topic of that assignment would be discussed in class on the day of class or before. So, during class, any questions or concerns you had about the topic, there was an opportunity to get an understanding about it. Same as with our parents, we were given instructions about having to do something and if our parents noticed we were not doing what we knew to do, they uttered the words "Get Busy!" God uttered these very words to me one day and from that day until now, I have been busy with the assignments He has given me to do. We all have God-given talents, gifts, and abilities for the purpose of fulfilling our purpose. Your talents, gifts, and abilities are tools to bring you wealth, joy, happiness, fulfillment, financial wellness, and purpose. But you have to get busy! Get busy with discovering what you're good at doing and find ways to maximize your potential. Get busy tending to your own business. Ecclesiastes 11:4-6 says, "Farmers who wait for perfect weather never plant. If they watch every cloud, they never harvest. Just as you cannot understand the path of the wind or the mystery of a tiny baby growing in its mother's womb, so you cannot understand the activity of God, who does all things. Plant your seed in the morning and keep busy all afternoon, for you don't know if profit will come from one activity or another, or maybe both." Get busy with that business plan you never completed! Get busy with the book you wrote but never published! Get busy with that song you recorded but never sang! Get busy with starting your own business! Why? Because you have what you need to start and finish! What are the things that are causing distractions in your life? The things for me were thoughts that I wasn't good enough. I wasn't confident enough to know I have what it takes to complete my dreams to the end. I wanted to have the step-by-step instructions on how I needed to do things. I wanted to know who are the people that will help me in the process? I would get frustrated by not having the money to do more and just frustrated by the whole process. The passage says we don't know how a baby grows in the womb. We just know the baby comes out healthy and whole. The Lord will work His miracles as we go forth in our assignments, so get busy!

Questions/Thoughts:

1. What are the "somethings" or "someones" distracting you from your assignments? Do you know what your gifts, talents and abilities are? If not, take the time now to discover what they are. There are different personality tests you can take to get to know yourself. I encourage you to seek them out.

NOTES:

_____

_____

_____

_____

_____

_____

_____

_____

_____

Wayward Children

Parenting children is a difficult task. I know there's a saying that parenting doesn't come with a manual, and though there isn't a step-by-step manual, the Bible is a guide we can use as a tool to help parents raise their children. I want to talk to parents whose children have moved out on their own and are waiting on God to answer prayers about their children. For those of you who have raised your children, have taught them to live moral lives, and taught them the meaning of purpose and giving back to their communities. For those of you who are waiting in faith to see the fruits of your labor, even for those parents who struggled raising your children and felt like you have slighted them, know that God will answer you. Just like God has a purpose and plan for your life, He has a purpose and plan for your children's lives (Jeremiah 29:11). The same God that will make things happen for your good is the same God who will make things happen for your children's good (Romans 8:28). Parents, you cannot get caught up in how your children are living their lives. You may see your children living in a way that is opposite of God's purpose for their lives, and you are fearful of what may happen. "Wayward" means difficult to control or predict because of unusual or perverse behavior.[12] "Perverse" means behaving in a way that is unreasonable or unacceptable.[13] So, a wayward child is a child that decides to live life opposite from what they were taught or learned. This can be a good or bad thing, but I want to talk to the parents that have raised their children with Godly morals and values. I want you to be encouraged that God saw how you stewarded over your children, and He will answer. The scripture tells us to train up a child in the way that he should go, and when he is old, he shall not depart from it (Proverbs 22:6). Parents, it is not your responsibility to control your child or children's decisions; our responsibility is to love our children, nurture their gifts, and live a lifestyle that's parallel to how God's word says we are to live. Now, I know all parents do their best with raising their children in how they were taught and raised. As parents, we all have to be retaught by God for

---

[12] wayward (yaktack.com)
[13] perverse (yaktack.com)

many reasons. Such as parenting out of fear, when this happens, we want to control our children. Parenting through a religious or legalistic lens can look like parenting in black or white. There is no gray area. In the story of the prodigal son, the scripture tells us that the son came to his senses when he realized he was living beneath his standards. The son knew where he came from; he knew he always had a fresh meal from the livestock they owned. He knew he had a comfortable place to lay his head. He knew his father loved him and was concerned for his life. The son also knew that he sinned against his father. The son knew he was living opposite of what he was taught. The son knew he did not steward well over his inheritance. Parents, we can identify with this son's father. We know some of our children don't steward well with what they have been given and even worked for. This also includes them stewarding well with their gifts, talents, and abilities. The scripture says the father was filled with compassion when he saw his son coming back to him (Luke 15:20). Parents, let's be the same. Let's be filled with compassion towards our children when we witness the change in their hearts and actions. Parents, let's welcome our children with open arms because we once were wayward in our living.

Questions/Thoughts:

1. Do you have children that you are praying to God because they are living contrary to God's best for them? If so, keep praying. The scripture tells us to pray without ceasing. (1 Thessalonians 5:16)

NOTES:

_____

_____

_____

_____

We Have Free Will

There is such freedom in having the ability to make choices. The definition of "will" means expressing desire, consent, or willingness.[14] Having this type of freedom is one of many reasons people want to move from third-world countries to the USA, all because of free will. People will make a choice to risk their lives facing death, escaping to the USA, so that they can express and live out their desires. God has given us free will. It all started in the Garden of Eden. God told Adam that he could eat from every tree except for the tree of knowledge of good and evil. One of the beauties of us having free will is the freedom to make a choice. But in having freedom, there are exceptions to the rules. Paul said in 1 Corinthians, "I am allowed to do all things, but not all things are good for me to do." God also tells us what a blessed life looks like and what a cursed life looks like, and though He encourages us to choose the blessed life, He gives us the freedom to choose (Deuteronomy 30:19). We have to remember this when it comes to our children or dealing with people in relationships. If you're a parent like me, once our children get to that stage where they can be on their own and they choose not to listen to our advice, we have to let them be. Now again, just because they can be on their own doesn't mean that they should. But if they don't want to adhere to the rules you set in your home and there is constant strife in that relationship, it's time to back up, especially if the children have moved out of the home. God will give us wisdom on how to deal with our children, but one thing we need to remember is that they have free will. Even in relationships outside of parenting, when a person is making a choice to leave or do something that will cause a break in the relationship and this is consistent behavior, we get to make a choice on what we want to do. The Lord freed my mind one day about nine years ago. I was struggling in my mind and heart one day about certain people who were close to me at the time, and I was worried about the choices they were making. I was trying to figure out ways I could make them see that their decisions weren't beneficial to them. God spoke so clearly to me, saying, "Don't

---

[14] Merriam-Webster. (n.d.). Will. In Merriam-Webster.com thesaurus, Retrieved from https://www.merriam-webster.com/thesaurus/will

go over anyone's choice!" "I don't go over yours, so don't go over theirs!" Those words quickened my spirit and have stuck with me ever since. Choices have consequences, good or bad. In a relationship, a person wants to be chosen, valued, wanted, respected, honored, and thought of. In our relationship with God, He wants the same from us. He wants us to choose life, which is choosing Him; He wants respect and honor. He wants us to show Him appreciation for who He is to us and what He's done for us. But He wants us to choose. He wants us to desire Him. He wants us to do these things willingly. Why? Because it means more. It shows it's genuine. It shows our acts are not forced. It grieves God's heart when we don't do things His way or when we make Him our last choice. Ouch! I encourage you to allow people their free will. You are not responsible for anyone's choices; they are!

Questions/Thoughts:

1. Do you struggle with allowing people their free will? If so, why? Are you experiencing negative consequences due to being in connection with someone for the choices they made? If so, take it to God in prayer and ask Him for wisdom on what to do because if it's hindering your purpose, you can make a choice to do something about it!

NOTES:

_____

_____

_____

_____

_____

Generosity

We have a duty to be generous to our neighbor. If anyone has a brother or sister in need but has no pity on them, how can the love of God be in that person (1 John 3:17)? I have helped family members, friends, and church members stay in my home at different times throughout my life, free of charge. One thing that helped me decide to help them and allow them to stay in my home was thinking if something happened to my children and they needed help, the seed would be sown. Also, I couldn't imagine being homeless and needing a place to stay. Thankfully, I have always had my own place since I moved out of my mother's home at the age of 18, and I have struggled and know what it's like to have little. I remember being without a car, having to walk to the store or call someone for a ride to get to work, having to depend on someone else. Our resources don't belong to us just to take care of our families, but it's for our neighbor, whoever fits the description of needing help. Luke 10:35-37, the man asked Jesus a question, "Who is my neighbor?" And Jesus told the man a parable about a man being robbed, naked, and beaten, and how three different people had the opportunity to help him, but it was the one who showed mercy to the man that mattered to God. This is how we should be, merciful in our deeds and attitudes. We like to ask questions about how a person got in the position they're in, and none of that matters when a person is hurting. They need their wounds addressed first, then we can deal with helping them make better choices that lead them up to that point later, if we get the opportunity. One of the synonyms for the word generous is open-handed. In order to share, we have to be open-handed with our resources. Hebrews 13:16 says, "And do not forget to do good and to share with others, for with such sacrifices God is pleased." When we give, it will be given back to us in whatever measure we give. When someone had a need, I was open-handed with my time, my finances, my home, my food, my cars, clothing, and my knowledge; any resources I had to share, I did. Did I feel jolly about helping all the time? No. Did I complain at times? Yes. Did I make those people feel less than because of their situation? Well, maybe my daughter! Did I ask those that I helped to remember me when they got on their feet or to pay me back? No. Did any of those people I helped do for me what I did for them? No. Did I always have in my overflow to help those in the capacity I helped? No. There were times things got pretty tight, but God allowed me to work overtime at my job, and somehow He made a way. God can't lie about His word. He will supply all of our needs according to His riches in glory by Christ Jesus (Philippians 4:19). Don't let what you need stop you from being open-handed with your resources to others in need. God sees you, and He will reward you for your generosity.

Lord, I pray for those who are open handed with the resources you have blessed them with towards others in need. I ask you to open the windows of heaven and pour them out a blessing, they don't have room enough to receive (Malachi 3:10). I ask you to increase the work of their hands, and declare they will always have more than enough to give. I ask you to ease their worries and any concerns they may have. It's your will that we share in others burdens (Galatians 6:2). In Jesus name Amen!

Questions/Thoughts:

1. How can you show generosity to others?

NOTES:

_____

_____

_____

_____

_____

_____

_____

Betrayal

Betrayal is a hard circumstance I believe we all have experienced in our lives. Betrayal is a violation of a person's trust or confidence of a moral standard.[15] So when someone cheats you, lies to you or befriends you for their gain, that is a painful experience. Jesus experienced betrayal by Judas, one of his disciples that he chose to be on his team to win. Judas had an opportunity to glean from Jesus and his power, to use it to teach others and to bring healing to the world. Instead he allowed ill intent in his heart and chose to be the one to betray Jesus and have him arrested to be crucified. What Judas didn't know is God knew all along and had a plan for Jesus to be the sacrifice for the world's sin. God turned a horrible, painful moment into a victory. Jesus knew at the last supper with the disciples who would betray Him and told the disciples I know the one that has ill intent towards me (Matthew 26:21). I can remember a time being betrayed by an ex in a relationship and before the explosive moment of me confronting him. I knew what was going on because there were signs. When I gathered enough evidence, I confronted my ex and the rest is history. But the pain, shame and embarrassment I experienced was breathtaking. I was so hurt and broken by that betrayal. I believe Jesus felt the same brokenness and pain which is why he went to pray in the garden of gethsemane. I also believe this betrayal was a little different. Jesus knew that he would be betrayed by his own and had to experience a painful death. For most of us, our betrayal takes us by surprise. If I were to know that connecting in that relationship, being cheated on, lied to, getting pregnant and him marrying another woman while we were supposed to be engaged and together, would happen, I wouldn't have opened that door. That was humiliating. That was the ultimate betrayal. It was unnecessary to do something like that. I couldn't imagine hurting someone like that. I know that you have been betrayed and you may be experiencing the repercussions of that betrayal now. I want you to know that you can recover from that betrayal like Jesus did. God can cause that pain to work for your good. Don't allow those experiences to cause you to park in bitterness

---

[15] Merriam-Webster. (n.d.). Betrayal. In Merriam-Webster.com thesaurus. Retrieved from https://www.merriam-webster.com/thesaurus/betrayal

and resentment. Learn the lesson and move on from that. If you are the person that caused the betrayal, repent and seek out recompense. Ask God to show you what you can do. If you can't make it right. Tell God about it, ask for forgiveness and allow Him to heal you. The person that caused the betrayal and the one that betrayed can be healed, set free and delivered.

Questions/Thoughts:

1. Have you been betrayed? Are you healed from that experience and able to move on from it? Do you harbor unforgiveness in your heart from what happened to you? Ask God to heal your heart and turn that pain into a victory.

NOTES:

_____
_____
_____
_____
_____
_____
_____
_____
_____
_____

What's the Reason for the Hope You Have?

Human beings have a choice to hope in many things, but the reason for my hope far outweighs what this earth can bring me. My concern is not just for the external things but the internal things: joy, peace, contentment, favor, strength. These are things money can't buy and willpower alone can't produce. The reason for the hope I have is because of what Jesus Christ did on the cross for the world. My mind can't fathom such a sacrifice. I love that we, especially Christians, get the opportunity to share why we put our hope in Jesus Christ. This is an opportunity to share why we believe in Him and why we put all of our hope in Him. I believe and put my hope in Him because I know that will or chance alone did not pull me out of the dark valleys in my life. I believe and put my hope in Him because I know the blessings I have been able to attain did not just come from hard work alone. I believe and put my trust in Him because I know my soul needs to be saved. I'm looking forward to the day where all of the turmoil that we are experiencing on this earth will be over! I also know in the meantime that I have been given a promise to live an abundant life now instead of waiting, so I choose to take Him at His word. The scripture tells us to be ready to share your reason for the hope you have. So this means your experiences, your troubles, your opposition will give you opportunities to share with others why you haven't given up on your hope, your faith, given up on your family, and given up in life. James 1:2-4 says, "My brothers and sisters, when you have many kinds of troubles, you should be full of joy, because you know that these troubles test your faith, and this will give you patience. Let your patience show itself perfectly in what you do. Then you will be perfect and complete and will have everything you need." When we are afflicted, it is for others' consolation and salvation (1 Corinthians 6). Our trials are not to keep to ourselves; they are to share, and this is what gives others hope. When we endure the trials and tribulations, this is what produces our hope. For hope is trusting in something or someone. Hope is having an expectation in something or someone. I'm sure we all have experienced by now that life circumstances are temporary and human beings are fickle. But one thing that is sure is Jesus and all His majesty! My prayer for you is that you open your heart to the truth of what this hope is and allow Jesus to super exceed your expectations about this hope He promised us.

My reasons for the hope I have

I became a single mother at age 16, got pregnant again at age 17 but had an abortion. By the time I was 22, I had another child, unwed. Up to that point in my life, I experienced toxic relationships with men. My father was present in my life but he was not a hands-on supportive father throughout my childhood into most of my adulthood. I experienced a male relative and pastor touching me inappropriately as a child and teenager. I was able to graduate high school and have worked since I was 14 years old. I got my own apartment at 18 and have been on my own ever since. I married, and that marriage ended in divorce in a short time span. I raised my children as a single parent with help from their fathers, which means my children experienced blended families. I pursued a college degree in 2001 and have attained an MSW in 2020. I know what it is like to receive public and community assistance, standing in lines for food and Christmas drives. I experienced traumatic experiences in my relationships that caused me to go into depression. My daughter became a teenage parent at the age of 14 and another by the age of 21, and she has experienced a lot of the same situations I have as a single parent, toxic relationships, depression, and struggling to navigate being a single parent. Through all of this, my daughter and I have made it through and are still making it through. Through all of this, God has provided for me beyond my understanding. I was offended with Him in a few of those seasons. I blamed God for how I was being mistreated by others. I had to learn that my affliction would be hope for someone else's affliction. For my daughter to be exact! She knows most of my story and saw me navigate through those difficult times, and she will testify that my hope in Jesus is what saved me, pulled me out of those horrible pits, out of the miry clay, and set my feet on a firm foundation as He established my goings. He will do the same for you! (Psalms 40:2)

Questions/Thoughts:

1. What is your hope in and why? Have you heard about putting your hope in Jesus Christ and what this means? If not, ask God to allow you to believe in and experience this hope. Your life will never be the same!

NOTES:

Don't be Afraid of Rejection

Why are so many people afraid of rejection? If I'm honest, I struggle with this at times. Rejection means to dismiss or refuse something, to turn down.[16] No one wants to be turned down. We all want acceptance because this is a part of our human makeup. I believe that our traumatic experiences in childhood shape how we deal with rejection. Most of my experiences with rejection have been negative. I internalize rejection as "I'm not good enough," which I believe most do, and this may stem from the unhealthy situations or circumstances we have encountered. If someone is calling you out of your name, using profanity at you while they are telling you they don't want to be with you, you would internalize being rejected in a more negative way than if someone says, "I need to share something with you, and I know it's not going to be easy to hear. I have been feeling like this for a while now, and I think it's time for me to move on from this relationship due to [fill in the blank]." The first way was demeaning and disrespectful. The second way was respectful and honest, and though telling someone that a relationship is ending would be hurtful for many reasons, you can consider the fact that they thought about what they were going to say and considered how you would feel. I believe we all need to be healed from past traumatic experiences so that when we hear the word "no" or feel like we are being dismissed, we will not have a negative feeling about it and go down this emotional pit. I also believe healing is key to our emotional growth because when our plans don't fit with God's plans, we tend to translate God's "no" to Him rejecting us. One thing God is not doing to His children that are pursuing Him and seeking out purpose is rejecting us. The scripture tells us that God is not like man; He doesn't think like man thinks, and He doesn't have ill motives like man does (Numbers 23:19). God's heart is pure towards us. God's "no" is His protection for us. He knows the plans that He has for us; they are not plans to harm us but to give us hope and a future (Jeremiah 29:11). Many are the plans of man, but the Lord's plans will prevail (Proverbs 19:21). I want to encourage you to look at

---

[16] Merriam-Webster. (n.d.). Reject. In Merriam-Webster.com thesaurus, Retrieved from https://www.merriam-webster.com/thesaurus/reject

rejection in a different way. If the relationship ends, rejoice! If the job does not hire you, rejoice! If the college you applied for did not accept you, rejoice! If you were turned down for the loan, rejoice! Are you following me? Rejoice in all things (Philippians 4:4)! You don't have to question if you're good enough, if you're pretty enough, if you have enough, or if you are enough when someone tells you "no" or you feel dismissed. Just continue on your healing journey, maximize your opportunities through your gifts, talents, and abilities, and watch how God opens up doors for you that no man can close (Revelation 3:7)! I'm a living witness.

Questions/Thoughts:

1. Do you struggle with being rejected? If so, I want you to reflect on the reasons why you are struggling. Ask God to heal your heart from your negative experiences and help you see rejection work for you instead of against you.

NOTES:

_____

_____

_____

_____

_____

_____

_____

_____

God Doesn't Show Favoritism

We live in a world where we all have our favorite things, people, or places we love. We have a favorite food, a favorite TV show we like to watch, a favorite person we like to listen to, a favorite type of book we like to read, certain people we like to be around, and a favorite vacation spot we like to go to, and the list goes on. "Favorite" means preferred before all others of the same kind or a person or thing that is especially popular or particularly well-liked by someone.[17] I'm pretty sure we all had an experience where we have been the person that was shown favoritism or been the person watching others being preferred over us. Maybe it was a job promotion you were offered because you had a good relationship with the person doing the hiring. Maybe as a child, your other siblings were favored over you because your parents noticed their achievements more than yours. Maybe you were voted most popular in school because of the way you dressed or had a charming personality. There are many reasons people have favorites, and that is totally fine as long as there is no malicious intent. What I mean by malicious intent is, "I'm choosing to be with this person over that person because I can relate to or connect better with this person," versus thinking, "I'm choosing to be with this person because I think they are better than the other person." When it comes to favoritism, people have their preferences, and though I believe this is fine, it can lead to insecurities towards others. With God, we don't have to worry about Him having or showing favoritism to His children. God does not prefer one child over the other. He prefers us all. He loves all of His creations. We all start at the same playing field with grace, favor, love, provision, protection. I love Romans 2:11 (AMP), "For God shows no partiality, no arbitrary favoritism; with Him, one person is not more important than another." The Message version 2:11-16 says, "If you go against the grain, you get splinters, regardless of which neighborhood you're from, what your parents taught you, what schools you attended. But if you embrace the way God does things, there are wonderful payoffs, again without regard to where you are from or how you were

---

[17] What (in English language) is the difference between 'favorite' and 'preferred'? (n.d.). Quora. https://www.quora.com/What-in-English-language-is-the-difference-between-favorite-and-preferred

brought up. Being a Jew won't give you an automatic stamp of approval. God pays no attention to what others say (or what you think) about you. He makes up His own mind." Well, you might ask, why do certain people seem to be more blessed than others? My response to that is when people obey God's way of living, they get rewarded for that. Also, though we all start off at the same playing field with God, people that have positions of authority, whether being parents, politicians, church clergy, or government officials, may have a different perspective about God and how we should live, which can cause discord in the original plan that God has designed, such as doing things and treating people from a place with love. For the person that has always been looked over, know that every word of affirmation that God has spoken in His word is for you and about you. Start living like you believe it!

Questions/Thoughts:

1. Do you have any negative memories about favoritism? Are you a person that has been looked over and others are always being preferred over you? I want you to know that God does not think like man. I want you to know that you are God's masterpiece.

NOTES:

_____

_____

_____

_____

_____

_____

Miracle Moments

Miracle moments are all around us. Most people, when they think of a miracle, may automatically think about something drastic happening, such as someone who is blind being prayed over and suddenly seeing, or someone in a wheelchair who can't walk getting prayed over and then being able to stand and walk again. These types of miracles are often referred to as "laying on hands." I used to think like this as well. When I heard the word as a younger Christian, about how we have power like Jesus to perform miracles, I thought something was wrong with me when I didn't see immediate results after praying and fasting over people with disabilities, mobility issues, or just needing God to turn their situations around. I had to learn that those types of miracles do happen, but that's not the only way they happen. Also, I learned that you have to have a relationship with God and allow that relationship to develop through faith. I came to understand that there are many factors to receiving miracles, which is why some are instant and some are not. Despite this, I have learned to see that miracle moments are all around us. A miracle is something supernatural, a wonder, or a phenomenon. So, when you think of these terms, a wonder is something that causes amazement. When you consider how a plane is designed and able to fly in the sky, that's amazing. When you think of how a ship is created and the weight of it, it's a wonder how it can sail on the water and be used as transportation to carry cargo, food, and whatever supplies we need for consumption. It's amazing to see how the clouds sit in the sky and how the rain is formed, and how the elements of Earth produce the right atmosphere for all the seasons and the different temperatures we experience in each season. I want to share some wonders I have experienced in my life. I remember driving one day while running errands. I ended up turning down the wrong street and was frustrated about it. As I was driving, I saw a "for rent" sign. Let me rewind a bit. During this particular time in my life, I was looking for a one-bedroom apartment because I needed to downsize from a three-bedroom home. I needed my rent to be at least $350 and no more than $400 a month. I did not believe that I could find a nice place in a nice neighborhood for this amount, but I prayed to God about it, even though I ended up searching for places that were well over that budget, with places I found being at least $550. So, fast forward back to seeing the "for rent" sign. The amount said $360, and pets were welcomed. I instantly called the number and spoke with the owner. He explained the stipulations to me, and I asked to see the place. Once I viewed the place, I knew it was mine. I immediately told him I wanted it and did the necessary things to secure the deposit. That was a miracle moment. I found a one-bedroom apartment in a nice neighborhood with a washer and dryer hookup for $360, and water was included. I have experienced so many other miraculous moments in my life, and I'm sure you have too. The scripture says, "Let the whole world fear the LORD, and let everyone stand in awe of him" (Psalms 33:8).

Questions/Thoughts:

1. Can you look around and see the miracle moments in your life? Are you amazed at what God has done for you in your life? If not, I pray that you have an encounter with God that will change your life forever and pray you will testify of his amazement in your life.

NOTES:

_____

_____

_____

_____

_____

_____

Pursuing God

Pursuing God is something we must do if we want to know Him. Knowing God and knowing about God are two different things. In order to know someone, you have to spend time with them. You can know of someone by hearing things about them through what someone has said about them or through reading something about them. You can learn about a celebrity or public figure through hearing the news, reading about them in magazines, books, or social media platforms, but you never really know them because you haven't spent time with them. You only know what you see or hear. I remember growing up in church as a little girl. We were in church at one point six days a week. There was always a program going on. If it wasn't my church home having service, it was a visiting church in the community that was having a service. I remember hearing the preacher preach stories about Paul and Silas, about Jesus coming back to get us. I remember being in Sunday school and learning about Jonah and the whale, Noah and the ark, and Mary Magdalene, how she washed Jesus' feet with her hair. I even remember being a part of the death, burial, and resurrection Easter play as a child. I played Mary Magdalene, telling the people that "He has risen!" So as a child, I knew of Him because of all of these experiences, but it wasn't until I started to seek out who I was, and seek out my place in this world that I would get to know Him. My experiences in life drove me to seek out this God I learned about as a child. I would hear and read that He is the great I AM. I would hear and read that He is a healer. I would hear and read that He is a provider. So, I started praying to God. I started fasting so that I could learn His voice. I purchased commentaries and Bibles with different translations so I could get a better understanding of what I was reading. Instead of just going to church and hearing a sermon, I sought out a relationship with God. The word "pursue" means to follow, seek, or engage in. If you want to know who God is, you have to follow Him, seek Him, and engage in a relationship with Him. Look at pursuing God the same way you pursue a career, a romantic or business relationship. When you pursue those things, you seek out what you want to do. You begin to invest your time to learn different skills and to gain knowledge. You invest your money in materials that you need to aid in your learning and growth. Lastly, you don't give up until your goals are reached. When you're in a relationship, you have to be supportive and committed to the process to help nurture the relationship. The scripture tells us to ask, seek, and knock, and the door will be opened (Matthew 7:8). God says, "You will seek Me and find Me when you seek Me with all your heart" (Jeremiah 29:13). Another scripture says, "Draw near to God, and He will draw near to you" (James 4:8). These words are promises. They are guaranteed. God is not a man that He should lie (Numbers 23:19). I can testify to seeking God and finding Him. It's a beautiful experience.

Questions/Thoughts:

1. Do you know about God, or do you know him? When was the last time you spent time with God that required you to invest and give?

NOTES:

_____

_____

_____

_____

_____

_____

_____

_____

Resolve It

What dispute or issue do you need to resolve in your life? What is causing contention in your relationships? What do you need to do or refrain from doing in order to resolve the problem(s) in your life? "Resolve" means to settle or find a solution to a problem, dispute, or contentious matter. It means to decide firmly on a course of action.[18]

When we don't resolve issues in our lives, they linger and fester until something or someone explodes. Nothing just happens. Unresolved issues cause contention, tension, stress, and distress. Abraham made a wise decision to part ways with Lot to get ahead of any issues that would arise as a result of their herdsmen having strife with each other due to their growing livestock taking up space. Abraham wanted to keep a healthy relationship with Lot, so he suggested they part ways to resolve their issue. Abraham said, "Whatever direction you pick, I'll go in the opposite direction and settle there with my livestock." They were able to resolve an issue before it got out of hand. Abraham did not want to ruin his relationship with his relative. Resolving issues shows maturity. How many stories do we know of families not being able to resolve issues, and they fester, causing arguments every time those family members are together, or it causes distance within those relationships? God is a problem solver, and He displays that throughout scripture. We should have problem-solving abilities just like God does. He tells us in His word, if anyone does not take care of his own relatives, especially his immediate family, he has denied the faith and is worse than an unbeliever (1 Timothy 5:8). He also tells us that if anyone is offended with their brethren, go and resolve the issue before bringing an offering to God (Matthew 5:23). God is love, and He wants us to display who He is to others. We should be able to resolve our issues with anyone if we say we are Christians. It's expected of us. I personally do not like strife, and I try my best to resolve those issues when they arise. I remember being owed $2000 dollars from someone, but I forgave the debt, not because I wanted to but because I wanted to keep the peace and move on from that lingering issue and all that

---

[18] "Resolve, V." Oxford English Dictionary, Oxford UP, September 2024, https://doi.org/10.1093/OED/4599856918.

came with it. When I was going through my divorce, I made sure I didn't hold any resentment due to the issues we could not resolve together. It was a respectful and peaceful divorce. Resolving issues with others is not easy, especially if you were the person that was not the cause for the issues. That's where maturity comes in. The scripture tells us we can do all things through Christ who strengthens us (Philippians 4:13). Whatever it takes, resolve it!

Questions/Thoughts:

1. How long are you going to ignore the issue(s) you need to address? This can be an issue with your physical, financial, mental health or a relationship you're in.

NOTES:

_____

_____

_____

_____

_____

_____

_____

_____

_____

Access Granted

If I were to ask you to pick five things that you would like access to, what would those be? For some of you, you may know instantly what those five things are; for others, you may feel five things aren't sufficient for what you need in your life. My response to that question would be the same. Five things aren't enough for what I need in my life. I need access to more in order to live an abundant life. The word "access" means to retrieve something or to enter a place.[19] Do you know that when a person becomes a believer, they transition from one realm of living to another? They leave one kingdom of living (earthly) for another (heavenly). Have you noticed that the way God wants us to live on this earth is the opposite of how heaven operates? The earthly kingdom says be independent. The heavenly kingdom says, "Lean not on your own understanding, but in all your ways acknowledge the Lord" (Proverbs 3:5-6). The earthly kingdom says if your neighbor mistreats you, they burn their bridges. The heavenly kingdom says, "Do good to those who mistreat you" (Matthew 5:44). The earthly kingdom tells us to save for ourselves. The heavenly kingdom says, "Give generously to others, and you will receive it back, pressed down, shaken together, and running over" (Luke 6:38). When a person becomes a believer, they gain access to enter this domain and all the benefits that come with it. A believer becomes the manager of the kingdom domain, just as citizens are managers of the earthly domain. So, you don't have to settle for access to only five things in life because you have access to all you need to live your life in abundance. You enter into a place of overflow, multiplication, joy, peace, healing, freedom, security, safety. You can retrieve mercy, grace, and the things we need for our daily living (Psalm 68:19). You will have access to create and to become owners of. These are all the things that people want in life. Access has been granted! A parent doesn't give a child keys because they know they might lose them, not understanding the value of those keys. A child doesn't understand that if they lose the keys to the house, the car, the business, or whatever the keys are

---

[19] access, v.2 meanings, etymology and more | Oxford English Dictionary. (n.d.). https://www.oed.com/dictionary/access_v2?tab=meaning_and_use

for, the parent will not have access, especially if there is no backup set of keys. Once those keys are lost, it causes hindrances and delays in gaining access to those places or retrieving valuable things that are locked up. I remember locking my car keys in the house while I was on my way to work one day. I was two and a half hours late for work, had to pay a professional to open my door, and had to purchase a new lock because that process caused damage to my door. Here I am with this nice shiny car that I couldn't drive until I had the keys to start it up. Once the believer understands the value of the access they have to enter and retrieve the things of the heavenly kingdom, they will begin to experience life in a different way.

Questions/Thoughts:

1. Do you know how to receive access to the heavenly Kingdom? If not, read Romans 10:9 and give your heart and life to Jesus. Practice building a relationship with Him and watch all the access you will receive as you can be trusted with God's kingdom.

NOTES:

_____

_____

_____

_____

_____

_____

_____

God's Love For Us Never Fails

We all should be able to testify to this truth that God's love never fails. How many times has He been there for us? How many times have we broken promises to God? How many prayers has God answered for us? The answers to all these questions are countless times. 1 Corinthians 13 tells us that love bears all, and that's what God did for us when He went  to the cross. God did not leave anyone out of the equation. He included our backgrounds, flaws, and did this all while giving us a choice to choose Him. Now that's love! He took on the world's burdens and sin and included us to have an abundant life and gave us a choice to choose Him. 1 Corinthians 13 tells us that love doesn't keep a record of wrongs. God doesn't hold us hostage to our failures and poor choices we make. Psalm 103:11-12 tells us that He will forgive our sins as far as the east is from the west. He tells us that He will throw them into the sea of forgetfulness (Micah 7:19). He tells us that He will remember them no more. I think this is a truth that human beings have a hard time believing. We condemn ourselves for our failures and harp on them. We deem ourselves unworthy of God's best for us. Where did this mindset come from? Because God doesn't think like this about us. God calls us His friends (James 2:23). God calls us a royal priesthood (1 Peter 2:9). God calls us His special people unto Himself (Deuteronomy 7:6). I believe this mindset came when the serpent convinced Eve that she had a right to access the fruit from the tree of knowledge of good and evil. Once she and Adam ate the fruit from this tree, they went and hid themselves and made leaves as clothes for their bodies, and God asked them how did they know they were naked (Genesis 3)? This mindset can come from disobedience, and it can come from us having an awareness about things in the world. Also, we associate good behavior with being rewarded and bad behavior with punishment. So when we have displayed bad behavior and rebel against what God has told us to do and how He has told us to live, we believe that punishment is what we deserve. Then here comes God and shows us nothing but love, uplifts us, and provides for us. This is what love is! And it's hard for us to fathom. I want you to begin to fathom God's love for you and start believing that you deserve it! For God so loved the world that He gave His only begotten Son just for you! He took the beating for you! He paid the price for you and that settles it!

Questions/Thoughts:

1. What can you do so that this truth can take root in your heart today? God's love isn't based on your behavior because if that was so, He would not have gone to the cross to die for our sins.

NOTES:

___
___
___
___
___
___
___
___
___
___
___

Moving Forward

The time clock was designed to move forward. Each day numbered on the calendar counts forward. When we read a story, it starts from the beginning of a certain event that took place to give us insight into how a person started and where they are now. These things, as they are, give us an indication of how we should move in life, and that's moving forward. The earth rotates forward day and night, no matter what is happening in the world. We, as believers, need to learn how to adopt this principle. Moving forward doesn't negate the pain or trauma you have endured or experienced. Moving forward doesn't negate experiencing each season in your life, whatever may have happened. Moving forward shows that, yes, I have a past, but it states I'm looking forward to the future. Paul said it perfectly and was specific about why: "I'm forgetting what is behind me and looking forward to what lies ahead" (Philippians 3:13). I believe Paul said this because he knew there was more to his life. Paul said that he wanted to know Christ and the power that raised Him from the dead (Philippians 3:10). Well, in our lives, we get to learn Christ's power through our experiences. Paul also mentioned, "This is for those who are mature" (Philippians 3:15). We are the ones that know the good, bad, and ugly will happen in life, but it won't stop our faith. Job said it best: "We can't just experience the good in life" (Job 2:10). An athlete's goal is to train for the ultimate prize, and that's winning the highest medal ever. I know an athlete doesn't apply all that training and discipline for 2nd place. Their mind is set to win 1st place. When they run, they don't look to the side or back to watch their opponent; otherwise, they would lose focus and momentum. It's the same with believers. When we focus on the problems, we lose momentum in our faith, praise, worship, and trust in God. But, when we decide to focus on the problem solver, the one who knows everything that we are going through, it continues to build our faith and gives us the power to stand in the midst of hell. It sends a message to the kingdoms of darkness that no matter what opposition is happening, God's power is greater. Learning how to move forward also causes us to be in expectation of what is to come. Because greater is coming. The scripture tells us our latter will be greater than our former (Job 8:7, Ecclesiastes 7:8).

The latest years of our life will be greater than the earlier years of our life. I'm sure there are many of us that are looking forward to that because those years didn't start off that great, but for many whose life did have a great start, God is saying forget that, "I have something even greater that you haven't seen, it hasn't even entered into your heart yet" (1 Corinthians 2:9). Some of you think you have experienced your highest moment in life and that it can't possibly get any better than that. Well, God says differently. If you stop moving or get stuck, you will never know. God's assignment never ends on this earth, and I believe because there is someone that will get stuck on this journey in their faith and deeds, so God gives the assignment to the one who will bring multiplication (Matthew 25:14-30). The one that stopped on their journey said it was too hard to move forward. That may be you today. I want you to know that God knows it's hard. He knew you would have weary days. He knew you would have sleepless nights. He knew you would feel lonely. And in all this, He says to take heart because He has overcome the world. I believe what God means by this, the things that are originally designed to break us, with His supernatural power, it will empower us, it will give us a fight-back spirit, we will overcome, and that will be the witness to the world about God's power in our lives. So, I want to encourage you today to get out of that rut in your mind, heart, and emotions. Stop saying, "those were the good old days", "they don't make days like that anymore". No! You won't experience a day in life like that anymore because no day or experience is designed to be the same. When we say phrases like that, we are feeling how we felt in those moments, the peace, happiness, joy, strength, excitement, satisfaction, contentment, connection, healthy relationships, and balance in life. Those are some of the emotions and experiences we remember that we long to have in every season. And we can! Move forward in your thinking, move forward in your actions. You have what it takes, and you have all it takes. Just move!

Questions/Thoughts:

1. Do you feel like you've lived your best days? I want you to know that greater is ahead if you allow God to be the driver in your life and circumstances.

NOTES:

Preserving Tradition

Tradition is something that has been in our world for thousands of years. Tradition is the passing of customs and beliefs from generation to generation.[20] Tradition is present in every culture, race, and community. Tradition is in just about everything we do. We see these traditions in weddings, funerals, and holiday gatherings. We see tradition at the Olympics in the lighting of the torch, and at every sports game, the American national anthem is sung. We see traditions in recipes for food passed down. We see traditions of family-owned businesses. Traditions are a staple in our societies. Tradition is part of our identity. Tradition is a reminder of who we are and where we have come from. Traditions are all throughout the Bible, from the way they celebrated festivals, to giving different offerings, the way people were buried, the certain attire they wore in the temples, to honoring a day of rest, to selective songs being sung, and the list goes on. As I get older, with my children living on their own in different states, and the majority of my family living in different states, I have struggled with how to preserve most of the traditions that I have become accustomed to when holidays come around. Easter, Thanksgiving, Christmas, and church are the most celebrated holidays and traditions that my family celebrates. We would pick a place to host the holiday and meet everyone there. In the last few years, not everyone has been able to show up for the holidays, and it's mostly due to our children growing up and having their own children and families, so they are making their own traditions. Now, I mentioned church being a tradition. I faithfully went to church service mostly every Sunday until COVID-19 happened. If I missed church, I was either out of town, sick, or working; otherwise, I'm there. These last few years I've been going less because I go alone, and to be honest, I feel alone. Going to church with my family is what I was used to doing, so I feel different. I'm thankful I am able to watch it on TV and most thankful for my foundation in my beliefs and relationship with God. I'm sharing this because you may feel alone as well, and I want you to know that God sees you, and He knows what you

---

[20] https://www.oed.com/dictionary/tradition_n?tab=meaning_and_use

are feeling. You may be experiencing changes in your family dynamic, and the traditions you're used to celebrating aren't the same for you, and you may feel alone because you're wondering, "Now what?" The children are gone, you're divorced or widowed. Family members have moved away and started their own families, or you may have lost loved ones, so it's not the same carrying on how things used to be. The dynamics of family will change, and we have to reinvent how we celebrate tradition and create new ways of preserving those traditions and seek out why it's important to us. 2 Thessalonians 3:6 (AMP) says, "And now, dear brothers and sisters, we give you this command in the name of our Lord Jesus Christ: Stay away from all believers who live idle lives and don't follow the tradition they received from us." Paul didn't want the Thessalonians to be deceived by lawlessness and encouraged them to hold fast to the truth. In preserving tradition, we need to make sure it brings glory to God, uplifting others, and honoring others who have left a legacy of righteousness (right living).

Questions/Thoughts:

1. What traditions do you preserve in your family dynamic? Are these traditions orderly and integral? If your family's dynamic has changed how can you preserve the traditions that are important to you?

NOTES:

_____

_____

_____

_____

_____

Our Speech Matters

There are so many scriptures in the Bible that talk about how we should and should not speak. Our speech matters because this is how the world was formed, through God speaking (Genesis 1:3). Our words are a force that can produce life or death, good or bad, negative or positive things. This is why the Bible warns us on how to speak. James 3:1-12 says that  our tongue is like a fire and that it cannot be tamed by man. On one hand, we use it to curse people; on the other hand, we use it to bless God. Another scripture tells us that life and death are in the power of the tongue and those who love it will eat its fruit (Proverbs 18:21). Another translation says we will be rewarded for what we say and how we speak. So, it is safe to say that most of us have the life we have spoken, whether we intended how circumstances in this life have played out or not. I remember noticing how my speech was when I was really starting to get serious about Christ and my lifestyle. Most of my speech was critical, judging, speaking out of fear, and not sure of who I was. I remember people would complement me, and I was not able to receive them without pointing out something I thought was bad about myself. When I think about it, I don't even know where that came from. Maybe because I wasn't validated enough as a child. I know I didn't receive validation from my dad, and my mom, I can't remember, so probably not. I'm not trying to state anything negative against my parents; I'm just stating my experiences and outcomes because of them. So, as I began to grow in my relationship with God and through studying His word, He would remind me of who I am in Him and the authority He has given me. As I learned this, I exercised my authority and grew in my confidence in Him and what He could do through me and for me. I want to talk about how our speech can cause others to become stronger. Ephesians 4:29 (NCV) says, "When you talk, don't say harmful things but say what people need—words that will help others become stronger. Then what you say will do good to those who listen to you." In this world we are living in today, everyone seems to be on edge in their emotions, and how we speak can be the thing to push them over the edge or into a breakthrough. I'll choose pushing them into a breakthrough for 300, Alex, lol… We as a society, in every culture, have experienced enough harm from our childhoods into our adulthoods. Harm means damage or made less valuable. We all need a break because not everyone is and will be saved (Matthew 7:21). So, because of this, we need to be under God's protection, and we need to be the ones to have speech that shows who we belong to. Those who belong to God, our speech should be encouraging, uplifting, and the truth, which is becoming a lost treasure in this world. Our speech should not be critical, judgmental without love, and damaging. I want to challenge you today to think before you speak (James 1:19-20). If you do this, it could literally change the course of your life and someone else's.

Questions/Thoughts:

1. I challenge you to think about the words you want to say before they come out of your mouth. Will your words lift up others or tear down others?

NOTES:

_____

_____

_____

_____

_____

_____

_____

_____

_____

_____

How Does God Feel About How We Utilize Our Time?

One day as I was writing in my journal about my day and how excited I was about using my time to volunteer at a work event, I had this thought pop into my head and I wondered: How does God feel about how we as His children utilize our time? I thought He probably feels like parents feel with their children when they lay around the house,  play video games all day, or are on their phones all day. When children have no interest in wanting to go outside and play, or older children when they don't want to go to social activities with their peers, or utilize their gifts, talents, and abilities by trying out for different social clubs, sports at school, or other extracurricular activities that may be available to them and they don't have an interest in accessing them. Ahh! That's a good word: accessing. Do you know that God has given us access to the kingdom? Do you know that we are made in the image of God and we have creative abilities like Him? We have vocal abilities like Him! When my children did not access or pursue their full potential, I had feelings of frustration and fear. We all heard that an "idle mind is the devil's playground," and the scripture says, "a youngster's heart is filled with foolishness, but physical discipline will drive it far away." As parents or caregivers, we have experienced life and we are in charge of making sure we guide our children and nurture their gifts, talents, and abilities. We understand the importance of being a guide to point them in the direction of what to do, things to try so that they can discover what they are good at, what they are passionate about, or their likes and dislikes. As parents, we also understand that when children don't access the choices they have to pursue, they can begin to form unhealthy habits. This is important because habits create patterns and patterns create cycles. Let's be honest, we are on our children because we don't want them to be lazy, we don't want them to be lost, we want them to be productive citizens in the world. We want them to be happy. Also, we know that our children are a product of us. I shared earlier the feelings I experienced as I was parenting my children throughout the different stages of their lives. When I look back, I realized I parented out of fear. I became a teen parent at 16 years old. I learned about generational curses. I wanted to protect my children from becoming statistics in the world. I worried a lot when I saw them forming unhealthy habits. I had difficulty parenting in the adolescent stages of their lives. So, for these reasons, we set rules and encourage our children to try out different things to help nurture what's in them. So this is how I believe God feels. He has set a path for us and how to get there. We will discover most of this course through our gifts, talents, and abilities and as we go and grow in Him, He will give us all that we need (2 Peter 1:3). I encourage you to utilize your time well because it's not easy to break unhealthy patterns and cycles. Ephesians 5:15-16 advises us to make the most of every opportunity because the days are evil. Proverbs 6:9-11 is one of my favorite scriptures: "How long will you lie there, you sluggard? When will you get up from your sleep? A little sleep, a little slumber, a little folding of the hands to rest— and poverty will come on you like a thief and scarcity like an armed man." This is what will happen if you don't utilize your time well. If you just let life pass you by and stand by being passive about your obstacles and oppositions and wasting away your gifts.

Questions/Thoughts:

1. Take an assessment of your time. What are you doing with your time? Who are you doing it with? Does it connect with your purpose? Does it connect with short term and long term goals?

NOTES:

_____

_____

_____

_____

_____

Caregiving

One of the most selfless acts a person can do is taking care of someone who can't repay the favor. Whether they are taking care of a parent, family member, or their job is caregiving, it touches God's heart. "Anything you have done to the least of these, you have done it to me. Anything you refused to do for the least of these, you have refused to do for me" (Matthew 25:40). You may ask, who are considered the 'least of these'? The ones that are not able to clothe themselves, feed themselves, those that are sick and in prison that need care. Jesus called those types of people good because they are souls that are being cared for. When a person is cared for, it is an opportunity for them to see and know that God cares about them and their situation. Human beings have a responsibility to others. When Moses was 3 months old, his mother put him in a basket and into a river to hide him from being killed by King Pharaoh. Pharaoh's daughter happened to see a baby in a basket in the river and saved his life by taking him as her own child (Exodus 2). Moses became one of the most prominent leaders to lead God's people out of bondage. Pharaoh's daughter's act of compassion to preserve Moses' life from her father's decree to kill all newborn males caused a nation to be saved. It caused God's will to be carried out and caused the people to believe in the God of Israel at a time when they were losing hope, thinking they would not be freed from their bondages and oppression. Ruth was the daughter-in-law to one of Naomi's sons, but he passed away. Naomi lost both her sons and husband, so she told Ruth she was moving away, but Ruth wanted to go with her. Naomi did not want her to go because she was young and could start over and find another husband, but Ruth refused. Ruth decided to stay with her to take care of her and ended up finding another husband and had a baby (Ruth 1). So, in these two stories, we see the caregivers' compassion, sacrifice of their time and plans, bravery, and love for those they cared for, displaying God's heart. All the caregivers that feel hopeless and feel that your prayers are not being heard, I want to encourage you that God hears you. The Israelites had been oppressed and in bondage for 400 years, and God used Moses to free them. Naomi thought God had forgotten about her and became very sad to the point of losing hope, but Ruth's love for her gave her hope and helped her to see that she didn't have to be alone in her pain. Caregivers, you are supporting others through and in their pain. Know that God calls you good and you will be rewarded back with time, finances, and alignment in purpose as you continue to have God's heart as you care for others.

Questions/ Thoughts:

1. Are you a caregiver? What do you need God to do for you? The reward for caregiving is two sided. God will take care of you as you take care of others and your reward is eternal.

NOTES:

_____

_____

_____

_____

_____

_____

_____

_____

_____

_____

Bye Bye Fear

What are you fearful of? I want to let you know that you don't have to fear. I know that as human beings we are going to experience emotions of fear, but we can choose what to do with it. I choose on a continuous basis that fear will not have me in bondage. It will not have me at a standstill. Let's look at some people in the Bible that allowed fear to overtake them. Jonah! The Lord told him to go to the city of Nineveh and preach to the people against the evil they were doing. Jonah decided to run away to Tarshish, and on his way while on the boat, the Lord caused a great wind on the sea. The wind was so bad it caused fear upon the sailors; they were afraid they were going to die, so they began crying out to God. In the meantime, Jonah fell asleep, and the captain went to Jonah to ask him to pray to his God. They all cast lots to see where this wind came from and why, and the lot showed that Jonah was the cause of the trouble. Now you may ask, what is casting a lot? The primary reason for performing this act was to render an impartial, unbiased decision on important matters. This is what was used to settle disputes (Proverbs 18:18). So, the story ends with Jonah being thrown off the boat and the wind ceases (Jonah 1:15). Another person in the Bible that allowed fear to consume them was Adam and Eve. After they ate from the tree of knowledge of good and evil, they hid from God's presence. Now why would they hide if they didn't do anything wrong, and why would they have the thought they did anything wrong? They were not ashamed to be naked, and the moment they ate from the tree they were told not to eat from, their eyes were opened to their nakedness (Genesis 3:7). Lastly, I would like to talk about the twelve spies. They were sent to the land of Canaan, the promised land, to spy out the land for 40 days, and when they came back to give a report, they told Moses that the land was prosperous but the people in the land were bigger and stronger than them. Only two spies believed they could possess the land and the other ten feared that they couldn't (Numbers 13:27-33). How many people in your circle believe that you can overcome any obstacle? We know that number is on the lesser side that believe that we can. Fear is an unpleasant emotion caused by the belief that someone or something is dangerous, likely to cause pain, or a threat.[21] How often do we live in the belief that our obstacles are greater than what or who God says we are or can do? Three things we can learn from these stories: First, God is not going to change His mind about the assignment He has given you. Second, when you fail or fall short, you don't have to wear shame because it doesn't belong to you. The final thing you can learn is that you are going to always be outnumbered in your faith, but you can rest assured that God will be with you.

Questions/Thoughts:

1. What are you fearful of that you need to say goodbye to? What do you need to stand up to? Who do you need to stand up to?

NOTES:

___

[21] https://healingaction.org/fear/

Spiritual Warfare

Spiritual warfare is real. For those of you that don't know what this is, let me share with you. Spiritual warfare involves demonic angels that are fighting for our souls. When Lucifer was thrown out of Heaven, he took some angels with him, and they are the angels that are fighting to win souls to build up their kingdom. God has His kingdom in heaven, and the demons have their kingdom in hell. Isaiah 14:12 says, "How art thou fallen from heaven, O Lucifer, son of the morning! how art thou cut down to the ground, which didst weaken the nations!" And verse 15 continues, "Yet thou shalt be brought down to hell, to the sides of the pit." Lucifer's name was changed to 'adversary,' which means to contend with, oppose, or resist, which is what he wants us to do.[22] The adversary wants us to oppose God's word and His way in exchange for his way. He knows the place that he lost with God, so he is trying to get us to lose our place as well. This happens through the lust of the flesh, the lust of the eyes, and the pride of life (1 John 2:16). The scripture talks about flesh and spirit. These two things are at war all the time. Our mind, will, and emotions are at war with the spirit of God living within us (Galatians 5:17). Ephesians 6:12 says, "For our struggle is not against flesh and blood, but against the rulers, against the authorities, against the powers of this dark world and against the spiritual forces of evil in the heavenly realms." There are many other scriptures in the Bible that tell us about spiritual warfare and how we can overcome it. First, God has already overcome the world and defeated Satan. Second, God has given us a choice to choose life or death, and if we choose life, we have access to weapons and power from above. If you continue to read down in Ephesians 6:12-19, you will see the weapons we must possess in order to fight the enemy: truth, righteousness, peace, faith, salvation, prayer. This is the way you will wage war on the adversary and win. I'm pretty sure with just this little knowledge, you can identify some things that have happened in your life and now you know that it's spiritual warfare. I want you to know that you don't have to be afraid of what's going on; if you

---

[22] Merriam-Webster. (n.d.). Adversary. In Merriam-Webster.com dictionary. Retrieved from https://www.merriam-webster.com/dictionary/adversary

have given your life to Christ, you have access to these weapons. If you aren't saved, you can ask God to save you right now, and you too will have access. God has no respect of persons (Romans 2:11). He died for the world, and whoever decides to believe in Him will have everlasting life (John 3:16). That's His promise to us!

Questions/Thoughts:

1. Now that you know some of the ways we are instructed to fight our adversary, what do you need to change in order to experience victory over the enemy in your daily life?

NOTES:

___
___
___
___
___
___
___
___
___
___
___

Live An Honest Life

In today's world, do people really know what it means to be honest? It seems difficult to put our trust in others with everything that we hear and read in the news and media platforms. Having moral character seems to be a disease. Help us, LORD! "There is no one righteous, not even one; there is no one who understands; there is no one who seeks God" (Psalm 14:1-3).  People seem to follow what everyone else is doing, but God never changes. God hasn't changed, and what He requires of believers will not change. The scripture tells us to "Enter through the narrow gate. For wide is the gate and broad is the road that leads to destruction, and many enter through it" (Matthew 7:13). It's obvious by watching a person's character and the fruit they produce that they are choosing the road that leads to destruction. The scripture tells us that we will know a person by their fruit. We will know a person by the way they speak and live. A person who is not trustworthy and has no desire to change is a person that is on the road to destruction. The scripture tells us there are six things the Lord hates, seven that are detestable to Him, and one of them is a lying tongue (Proverbs 6:16-19). Since we are made in the image of God, we are to display the character of God, and one of God's character traits is truth. When a person is trustworthy, they are reliable, dependable, and bring a sense of safety and security in that relationship because you know you can count on them to weigh out decisions and do what is right. When God can trust His children, He gives them rule over people to tend to. When Jesus asked Peter three times if he loved Him, and Peter responded by saying yes, Jesus was asking him, "Can I trust you to take care of my people?" When we become believers, we become stewards of God's kingdom, and part of stewarding God's kingdom is having rule over a certain group of people. If we love God, we will take care of His people. We will do right by His people, but we must first be right ourselves. Moses was a trustworthy man whom God was able to trust with the Israelites and he lead them into the promised land. The Israelites relied on and trusted Moses so much that they only went to him for all of their disputes. Moses was judging disputes day by day from morning to night, and his father-in-law Jethro noticed that he needed help. Jethro instructed Moses to find some capable men who were God-fearing and who could be trusted to help rule over the people and judge their disputes (Exodus 18). Remember, "Whoever can be trusted with very little can also be trusted with much, and whoever is dishonest with very little will also be dishonest with much" (Luke 16:10-12).

Questions/Thoughts:

1. Are you a trustworthy person? Do you know that your influence and gifts are to serve others? What would someone say about your character? Did you know that you are responsible for how you lead others?

NOTES:

_____
_____
_____
_____
_____
_____
_____
_____
_____
_____

Broken Hearted

The word "brokenhearted" takes my mind back to some dark places in my life. Before the age of 18, I experienced living in a single-parent home and not being raised by my dad. My sister and I often visited with my dad, and we have some good memories of things we did together, but I can't remember being protected by my dad. I can't remember him  supporting me when I became a single parent. I can't remember any father and daughter talks about life because it didn't happen. I remember being touched inappropriately by a pastor and a male family member. I became pregnant at age 15 and had my baby at age 16, and when I was able to move out on my own at age 18, I did. I often think about how my life would have gone if my father had been present financially, emotionally, physically. If he would have taught me about life and what I should expect from a man. Most of my male relationships I experienced by the time I was 21 had been betrayal, hurt, painful, distrust, manipulation, abandonment, rejection, and just toxic, to say the least. By the time I turned 22, I started to assess my life to see why I was experiencing such pain. Why would these men want to bring harm to me and take me through these painful experiences? These experiences had started to take root in my heart, causing resentment, low self-esteem, and questioning my value as a woman. I even had thoughts of not wanting to live. I didn't understand at the time, but I knew to turn to God, which is all I could do. I remember experiencing depression. I didn't take any calls except for one close friend. I remember not taking a bath for three days and hearing voices, thinking people were in my apartment. I cried so much at that time in my life! I cried! I cried! and I cried! I was so hurt, angry, and confused. I told God if my situation doesn't change, then take my life now because none of this is making sense, and I want out! I remember playing the Kirk Franklin song on repeat, "It's Over Now," and now that I'm reflecting back on that moment, that song was prophesying to my situation. I had the song playing for 3 days on repeat because I had no words for the pain I was experiencing. I'm more than sure that some of you can identify with what I'm talking about. That pain and all the emotions that come with it. On that third day, God pulled me out of that deep pit, and I have been changed ever since. That was the summer of 1997, and the rest is history on how God ordered my steps to my purpose from that moment on. I want you to know that God knows your heart is broken, and He has a plan to heal you and rescue you. Psalm 34:18 says, "The Lord is close to the brokenhearted and saves those who are crushed in spirit," but I love the Message version, "If your heart is broken, you'll find GOD right there; if you're kicked in the gut, He'll help you catch your breath." This is how I felt, kicked in the gut by hurt, pain, rejection, abandonment, and betrayal. I know you wonder how much more you have to take before the pain ends? I urge you to cry out to God and spare not (Isaiah 58:1). Tell Him how you feel. Tell Him what you want, ask Him to deliver you and give you direction. He understands you!

Questions/Thoughts:

1. Do you believe you can be healed from your broken heart? Have you taken an assessment of your situation? Are you ready for a change in direction? Turn to God right now in this moment and ask Him to come to your rescue. He made you a promise so take Him up on it!

NOTES:

_____

_____

_____

_____

_____

_____

We Are Protected

Do you know that we are protected by God? This world that we are living in is scary, to say the least. Sometimes, I wonder why the Lord didn't destroy the earth by wiping it out with the flood again, but He had to keep His promise. The rainbow is a sign of that covenant, so here we go (Genesis 9:11). People are trying to take the responsibility of protecting themselves and providing for themselves into their own hands, but we don't have to do this on our own. As a parent, we can see danger before our children see it. It happens with nature as well. God has naturally designed us to be this way, but there is a limit to our protection. He is El-Shaddai, God Almighty; He is Jehovah-Jireh, our provider. He is Jehovah Shammah, the one who will never leave or forsake me. God is true to Himself. He has to keep His word for His name's sake. Let's take the pressure off of ourselves and give it to the One who can handle it. He tells us that "there will be tribulation in the world, but take heart", because I have overcome the world" (John 16:33). That's good news. The Lord already knew that the world would be in a state of great trouble and suffering, but He told us to have joy in knowing He got us. I'm not gonna worry about planes crashing, shootings, robberies, car accidents, hurricanes, tornadoes, flood rains, and all the other evils and disasters that are happening around me because God knows, and He has already made provision and provided protection from it. He tells us a thousand may fall at your side, and ten thousand at your right hand, but it will not come near to thee (Psalm 91:7). He says that He is our shield and buckler (Psalm 91:4). He says that He never sleeps nor slumbers, so why shall I stay awake at night wondering and worrying (Psalm 121:4)? God tells us not to worry about our life, what we shall eat or drink, or what we shall wear because He takes care of the lilies in the field and sparrows in the sky (Matthew 6:26-30). That sounds good to me. I'm learning to rely upon God and give Him all of my cares because He can handle it. I have so many testimonies of God's protection, but I'll share the most recent one. I was boiling water to make some tea and went to my room and got on the phone and totally forgot about it. I woke up the next morning to get ready for work, and when I went to find the remote for my garage, I noticed the pot was on the stove still burning!

No smoke! No fumes! As if the stove was not on. I was in total shock. I hurried up to turn the stove off and jumped back in awe and just stood in the kitchen for a few minutes. Afterwards, I began to thank and praise God for His protection because this story could have gone another way, and I wouldn't be writing to tell you about it. I'm getting chills and excited now because our God is so good and amazing; He does great things for us. The stove burned from 8:00 pm to 8:30 am in the morning. I had a grease pot on the stove too! I make it a habit to declare God's protection over me, my children, my possessions, my children, and loved ones, and so far, so good. Guess what? So can you!

Questions/Thoughts:

1. List a few times God protected you. Know if He did it before, He can do it again.

NOTES:

_____

_____

_____

_____

_____

_____

_____

_____

Lies We Believe

The definition of a lie is to present false information with the intention of deceiving, to convey a false image or impression.[23] How many false images have we created in our minds about who we are and about who God is? How much false information are we hearing and reading on a daily basis that is shaping our beliefs? There has been a new phrase being stated by people in these last several years called "my truth." People have been claiming things and declaring false statements as living "their truth." There are a lot of false images and impressions in our society claiming to be true when it really is a lie. This deception started with Eve when Satan deceived her by twisting God's words, telling her that God didn't really tell her not to eat the fruit from the tree of knowledge of good and evil. Eve's reply was correct until she kept listening to Satan's deception and fell into the trap of eating the fruit. I remember the Lord clearly told me not to be in a relationship with a certain guy, and I tried my best to resist his advances, but he was persistent, and I ended up giving into his advances and being in a relationship with him. The turmoil I experienced in that relationship as a result of going against what the Lord told me not to do was something I regretted. I would hear the Lord's words replay in my mind constantly. When the Lord gives us instructions, it's for our protection. We think He is trying to hold things back from us. The scripture says, what father does not give his child good gifts? It also tells us that He will not withhold anything good from us (Psalm 84:11). How many lies have we believed that we are not good enough? That we are not called to do this? That we need this or that in order to make it? Too many times. Gideon is a man who believed he was the least of his family and that he couldn't defeat the Midianites with his people. He called his people weak. When the Lord looked upon him, He called him a mighty man of valor. God had a conversation with Moses, telling him that He heard the cries of His people and came to deliver them from their oppression, and told Moses to go and tell the people God is going to deliver them. Moses responded to the Lord saying, "Who am I to

---

[23] lie, n.1 meanings, etymology and more | Oxford English Dictionary. (n.d.). https://www.oed.com/dictionary/lie_n1?tab=meaning_and_use

approach Pharaoh, and who am I to lead Your people?" God told him, "I am sending you." What has God asked you to do? Who has God told you to bring deliverance to, or a word to, or a meal to? If God asked you, He qualified you. We don't need approval from the world or people. We believe the lies because we know our insecurities. We know the history of our generations and families. We know the educational background we come from. God knows all of this about us because He made us. The Bible says that He makes all things new. As we allow God in our lives, we change from glory to glory and faith to faith. We are like trees planted by the rivers of water, bearing fruit in every season. We become established, nourished, flourishing, and healthy beings. We become changed into the image of Christ. Let's believe in the One who is the way, the truth, and the life, and He will lead us into all truth.

Questions/Thoughts:

1. What lies have you claimed to be your truth? I encourage you to seek the scriptures of God's truth and practice speaking his words over your life daily until you see it manifest.

NOTES:

_____

_____

_____

_____

_____

_____

Rules and Consequences

If I were to ask you, do you like rules? What would be your answer? What if I asked you, do you like consequences? What would be your answer? My answer is yes to liking rules and yes to liking consequences if they benefit me. I believe most of us don't like the word 'rule' or 'consequences' because we view these through a negative lens. My guess is that most people relate rules to having restrictions, which is true, but rules are also considered boundaries or parameters. We cannot avoid having rules. There are rules in people's households, rules in culture, rules for driving, rules in marriage, rules at restaurants, rules at work, and the list goes on. 'Rules' means a set of regulations or principles governing conduct within a particular activity or sphere.[24] 'Consequences' are a result or effect of an action or condition.[25] So, the speed limit is 65. If you drive over that speed limit, depending on what zone you are in, you are bound to receive a fine. The consequences of driving over the speed limit cost you time taken away from where you were going that day, cost you money to pay for the ticket, and money to pay for court fees, not to mention the time you have to take out of your day to go to court. On the other hand, if you drive at the speed limit, you don't have to worry about your time being delayed or having to pay extra money for something you can avoid. So, rules and consequences aren't bad after all. If you do the right thing, you will reap the benefits. If you do the wrong thing, you will also face the consequences. Rules are for protection. Rules teach you maturity. Think about when your parents told you not to hang out with certain friends because their behavior and demeanor were negative. As a child, you thought your parents were being mean, but you found out they were right. God feels the same way about us as His children. The Lord has set specific regulations in place for our protection. These regulations will teach us how to be mature and responsible citizens. There is a conduct that we must display that mimics our Father in heaven. Galatians 5:22 lists the fruits of the Spirit: love, joy, peace, patience, kindness, goodness, faithfulness, gentleness, and self-control. The

---

[24] https://www.oed.com/dictionary/rule_n1?tab=meaning_and_use
[25] CONSEQUENCE | English meaning - Cambridge Dictionary

consequences of having this conduct and living this way will bring benefits of fulfillment, favor, and divine purpose. So, since rules are inevitable, would you rather do things God's way, or would you rather continue to do things your way? Either way, there is a result and a condition that you will receive. The choice is yours!

Questions/Thoughts:

1. Are you happy with the results of your decisions? If not, what needs to change for you to experience different results? Who are the people in your life that you continue to overlook their behavior? Are they adding to your life or purpose?

NOTES:

_____

_____

_____

_____

_____

_____

_____

_____

_____

_____

Freedom

Freedom is something everyone wants, and I want you to know that you can have it, but at a cost of being responsible. People are seeking freedom from mental anguish, freedom from physical pain, freedom from addictions and bondages, freedom from labels, and financial freedom. Though people want freedom from these things, God wants to give us freedom from what sin causes. John 8:34 says anyone who chooses a life of sin is trapped by it and becomes a slave to it. True freedom is living how God designs for us to live. God loves us so much that He gives us the freedom to choose how we want to live. He gives us the freedom to live for Him or live apart from Him. He doesn't control how we think. The scripture says, though we have the freedom to do anything we want, it doesn't mean that we should (1 Corinthians 6:12-13). There are consequences for living any way you want. If you live in the flesh, you will reap destruction, but if you live in the spirit, you will reap eternal life. Living in the flesh means living a life apart from God, which will lead to living in bondage (Romans 8:6). The scripture tells us that real freedom is living in the truth, and to find truth is to find God, and God is truth. We are the vines, and He is the branch, and anyone that lives apart from God will be cut off from Him. If a branch is cut or broken off from the tree that supplies its nutrients and causes growth, it will dry up and die, and there will be no use for it (John 15). If a believer decides not to live life God's way, they will die spiritually. God wants us to be like a child (Matthew 18:2-4). A child believes everything their parents tell them, no matter if what they were told did not happen at the time they said it would. A child never loses faith in their parents. A child will wait for that parent to provide what they said. A child is patient. A child is always in expectation of what their parents say to them. Freedom comes with responsibility. When a child becomes older, making friends, wanting to work and hang out, the parent begins giving that child freedom with the expectation that they will do what is right because this will determine how much freedom they can have. Our tests and trials and how we handle them determine how God can trust us and determine how responsible we are to handle what He has for us (Deuteronomy 8). When I was a teenager, I couldn't wait to get out of my mom's home and get my own place because I didn't like her telling me what to do. I thought I knew how to care for myself and make decisions for myself better than my mom. What I really wanted was freedom without restrictions, and freedom without restrictions is dangerous for anyone. There are reasons why an adult has to accompany a child under the age of 18. At the age of 25 is when a person's brain is developed enough to make concrete decisions, and depending on that person's experiences, it may take longer.

Questions/Thoughts:

1. What do you want to be free from? Do you believe that you can be totally free from bondages? Free from bowing to it!

NOTES:

_____

_____

_____

_____

_____

_____

_____

_____

_____

Persistence

Do you want to overcome adversity? Do you want to live the best life you can live? One of the ways to overcome adversity and to live the best life you can live is by being persistent. Persistence means to be continuous, firm, and resolute no matter what difficulty you are facing or no matter the opposition.[26] Being continuous means having no interruptions. There is adversity all around us, and there are plenty of opportunities to settle for what life brings us. There is a scripture that talks about how we need to accept our lot in life Ecclesiastes 5:19. The word "lot" means the condition of a person's life.[27] Though we all have something in our lives that if we had a choice, we would do without, we have to learn not to allow those certain conditions we encounter or experience to define who we are. We need persistence to thrive. We need persistence to live. You can't complete a goal without persistence. You can't have relationships and friendships without persistence. Most of all, we can't believe in God and have faith without persistence. The scripture tells us we only need a mustard seed of faith to move mountains. It's totally impossible for a human being to move a mountain with bare hands, but not for God. A mountain is a metaphor for opposition—everything that opposes who our faith says we are and what we can have. Luke 18:1-5 (MSG) tells us about a widow in the Bible who went before a judge and how she was persistent in asking for justice about an unjust matter. The scripture says this widow continuously asked the judge for justice until he granted her request. The judge didn't even want to do it, but he did it because the widow did not give in to him not helping her. She wouldn't take no for an answer. The judge being bothered by her request for help did not deter her from being persistent until she got the help she needed. Be persistent with loving those that are hard to love. Be persistent with making less money because tending to your family is what's most important now. Be persistent in your faith with the assignment God has called you to, no matter how tough it gets. God will hear your

---

[26] persistence, n. meanings, etymology and more | Oxford English Dictionary. (n.d.). https://www.oed.com/dictionary/persistence_n?tab=meaning_and_use
[27] Vocabulary.com. (n.d.). Lot. In Vocabulary.com Dictionary. Retrieved from https://www.vocabulary.com/dictionary/lot

cry for help, and He will grant your request at the right time. I remember living in a two-bedroom apartment, and I received a letter stating I was approved for a voucher to help me with rental assistance, but the place I was currently at did not accept this voucher, so I had to move. As I began looking for places, I saw this home that I became interested in wanting. I drove to the location of the home and saw the number on a sign and began to call it. I called daily for three weeks straight and left messages, but no one responded until the end of that third week of me calling. A lady answered the phone, stating she had received my messages, but her husband was in the hospital and wasn't able to get back with me. I told her about this voucher I had and asked if she accepted it, and she stated she hadn't done that before. She asked me how much the voucher was for, and I told her. The voucher was less than the market rental value and I asked her if she could go down $150 in rent so this voucher could work for me. After a few minutes of me pleading my case, she agreed to rent the place to me for $150 less than the original price. It was my faith in God and being persistent with calling that number that caused me to get the place I desired.

Questions/Thoughts:

1. What is it that you need God to do for you? What condition of life are you in that you need God to change it? I encourage you to be persistent like the widow. Don't let the no's of others affect what God is calling you to do and be.

NOTES:

_____

_____

_____

_____

Injustice

This world we live in is full of injustice. It's full of people who are unfair, corrupt, and it's full of inequality. When we hear of our political leaders, they make promises to address the inequality, unfairness, and corrupt behaviors in the world. Addressing these issues seems like an endless goal. Though there are times when things seem hopeless, we have to hold on to a glimmer of hope. The needle seems to move up in addressing these issues, then back, like an unbalanced scale. You may ask, what causes injustice, and my answer would be people's agendas. Not everyone has the same agenda as God. God's agenda is for everyone to act justly, love mercy, and walk humbly with Him (Micah 6:8). If we all did this, we would not hear of all the injustice that is going on in our world today. Thankfully, we can put our trust in God to uphold us in the midst of all the injustice that is going on. Now, this doesn't mean that we will not be affected by it or even experience it. I believe everyone will experience someone being unfair to them, inequality, and corruptness. Experiencing these things can cause a person to become bitter, angry, resentful, malicious, and harbor hatred in their hearts because of the pain and oppression it causes. When you put your trust in someone and they are unfair to you, it can cause damaged emotions. The important thing we have to remember is to learn to forgive. Jesus is a great example of experiencing unfairness, corrupt behavior, and inequality. Jesus was not guilty of any sin, but the pressure of the people made Pilate give in and declare an innocent man guilty of a crime he did not commit. Pilate had no evidence against Jesus but had evidence against Barabbas, who should have received the penalty for his crime (John 18:38). Psalm 9:8 tells us that God is a fair God. God is so fair that He took Barabbas' place to be crucified and die, and He died for the entire world. God allowed everyone to start at the same level playing field. Though we all start at the level playing field, God gives us free will to choose how we want to live and who or what we want to serve. You may be wondering what God is going to do about the injustice that is going on in the world? I have three responses to this question: the first is that people will reap what they sow. They will reap the consequences of their actions and choices, which can be many things. Second,

God wants people to realize how they are living and how their negative behaviors affect others, so He is patient with them to see if they will realize the error of their ways, like David did. David realized his lust caused him to kill an innocent man, and what he did to that man caused a curse to fall on him and his children (2 Samuel 12:9-14). Lastly, those that do not repent and turn from their sins will receive their reward, death, and separation from God for eternity (2 Thessalonians 1:9). I encourage you to receive God's invitation to live life according to how He has designed, so that you can reap the benefits.

Questions/Thoughts:

1. What is your response to the injustice, unfairness and corrupt behavior that is going on in the world today? My hope is that you are not a part of the problem but part of the solution. If not, I encourage you to repent today and make a choice to be a part of the solution.

NOTES:

_____

_____

_____

_____

_____

_____

_____

_____

Living Beyond Your Emotions

Emotions are an important part of our make up as humans and they are a person's response to an event or situation. The way a person responds to an event or situation depends on their different experiences. When a person has encountered a traumatic event their nervous system records that experience, and if anything remotely happens that mimics what that person felt during that experience it can trigger the same response as if the traumatic experience happened again. I used to work at a crisis center and any noise I heard at the center I had to respond to such as, if the doorbell or the phone rang. Anytime I entered in and out of a door, it made a noise. I had to carry a walkie talkie to respond to any communication about what was needed. If the clients elevated their voices, threw something or banged on the wall I had to respond to make sure they weren't hurting themselves or anyone. While working at the center, I had to be attentive to every sound because it could mean that I needed to address an issue. So, due to this heightened state my body experienced from all the different noises working this particular job, it affected me outside of work. One day I was out eating at a Mexican restaurant, and I ordered fajitas. When the waiter was bringing my food to the table I heard the sizzling noises, and saw the smoke from the food, so when I turned around to look where the noise was coming from, I instantly jumped as if there was danger present. My heart was beating so fast. Once I knew it was just my food, I was ok. That moment helped me realize how crisis work affected me. Many people live in a heightened state of emoticons daily due to their circumstances or environment. Some ways you can learn to live beyond your emotions and not allow your emotions to rule your life is being aware of why you feel the way you feel. Don't ignore what you're feeling. Explore what is causing you to feel that way and learn how to address it. Learn how to regulate your emotions. When a person doesn't have control over their emotions it causes disruption in relationships. It affects your mood and how you feel about yourself. Lastly, undealt and untreated emotions can affect how you make decisions. The scripture tells us to be anxious for nothing but to pray about everything (Philippians 4:6). If you ask God the reason for the way you respond to certain things that are not healthy for you or others, and ask Him to heal you, He will give you direction and wisdom on what to do (James 1:5). Don't allow fear, hatred, jealousy, envy and strife cause you to miss out enjoying your life and the relationships with people that are important to you. The prodigal son's brother had unhealed emotions against his brother when his brother came back home, and their father received him and threw a celebration for him. That should have been a joyous moment for everyone. His brother was living below his means and found himself in a desolate place but realized that he didn't have to live like that and made a decision to come home to his family and be surrounded by people that knew him and loved him (Luke 15:11). The father showed mercy and love to his son and the brother was jealous of that. What would cause him to feel like that?

Questions/Thoughts:

1. How do you deal with your emotions? Do you have an experience like the prodigal son's brother? Explore why you are feeling this way and ask God for wisdom on how to heal.

NOTES:

_____

_____

_____

_____

_____

_____

Encourage Yourself

One of the things that has gotten me through difficult seasons in my life or tough situations is encouraging myself. During those times, it counted most because I don't wear my problems on my sleeve. I'm a solution-focused person, so when I experience a problem, my brain goes to pondering how to fix it. There were times when there was no solution I could come up with to fix a cheating, non-supportive husband. There was no solution to fix my 14-year-old pregnant daughter. The only thing I could do was to cast those cares upon Jesus and ask Him to give me strength. I had to seek out scriptures in the Bible about forgiveness, love, embracing, and mercy. I had to combat every negative emotion I experienced and tell myself that "I am loved", "I am wanted by God and others that need me". I had to tell myself that "I am not a failure, but I am a wonderful parent". I had to tell myself that "this too shall pass". In the tough seasons of life, you have to learn how to encourage yourself because usually no one else is around when you are at your lowest, when you are at your breaking point. How often do we internalize our failures and mistreatment from others as something we did or didn't do? We have to remember that people have a choice. We have a choice too! We can choose to uplift ourselves in a bad situation or give in to the lies the enemy wants us to believe. David is known as the man who encouraged himself in the Lord. 1 Samuel 30:1-6 tells of a time about David and how his territory was invaded by the enemy. His city was burned by fire, and the women and children were taken captive. Due to this, the people that were with him began talking of stoning him because of what they lost, but the Bible tells us that David encouraged himself in the Lord. David had to think quickly. He was King, and he couldn't get caught up in the emotions of the moment. David knew who he served and knew the power he had. Just like David, you can do the same. You can make a choice to remember the God you serve and know the power that has been given to you. David was given permission to pursue the enemy and took back all that was lost (verse 8). One of my favorite scriptures is Psalms 42:5 (MSG), which says, "Why are you down in the dumps, dear soul? Why are you crying the blues? Fix my eyes on God; soon I'll be praising again." This passage is saying there is no reason to be down when you serve a God that will lift you up. I get it! And so does God when it comes to having your moments of expression, but don't park there—put that gear in drive and move forward in praise! Whatever tough situation you may be finding yourself in right now, I declare that you shall recover all. You will overtake the enemy of hate, jealousy, comparison, self-sabotage, lack, poverty, greed, lust, and you can fill in the blank. The scripture tells us that we are more than conquerors, we are overcomers, we are victorious! Believe it!

Questions/Thoughts:

1. What is causing you distress? What is causing you to be discouraged and down? Make a decision that you are going to deal with it! What are 3 things you can say out loud to yourself right now to lift you up?

NOTES:

_____
_____
_____
_____
_____
_____
_____
_____

A Thankful Attitude

Having a thankful attitude is a sign of maturity. People who are like this know that it is better to have a positive attitude about a bad situation or circumstance than to be negative about it. I don't like to drive in foggy weather because I can't see very well, especially at night, and if you turn on your bright lights, it only makes it worse, so it's best to drive slowly so you don't put yourself or others in danger. This is how it is when you have an ungrateful attitude. Your negative thoughts cloud your perspective, and you see life through a foggy lens. You then become toxic with your words, which puts you and others in danger. We can find a lot to be negative and ungrateful about, but Psalm 100:4 tells us to enter into His gates with thanksgiving and into His courts with praise; be thankful to Him and bless His holy name. When you visit someone's home that has a gate and walk in, you're walking onto their property. You're in their space, just the same as if you walk up to someone, you're in their space. Now imagine walking up to someone and starting to ask them to do something or start complaining about something; that would be considered rude. The proper thing would be to greet them first, then start sharing about your day or asking them for something you need. Have you ever gone to a grocery store, got up to the counter to pay for your food, and the cashier doesn't acknowledge you? They just take your money and move on to the next person! How rude is that? That happens to me most of the time when I go to a certain grocery store. I don't know what type of training they are doing, but it is not very good. Instead of having cameras on the people putting their groceries in their bags, they need to have cameras on their cashiers to improve their customer service. But I digress. My point is, when you walk into a person's space and you have negative energy, and you don't acknowledge them or greet them, that is being rude and disrespectful. So, when we come into God's presence and don't acknowledge Him, we start complaining about our circumstances and the people that are in our lives. That's entering into His gates the wrong way. God does not deserve that! He is the great I Am, and you can fill in the blank on who He is to you. Reverence is the way we must enter when we come into His presence. What parent, you know, will allow their children or children that are not theirs to demand things from them and complain to them without consequences? We have to learn to think in a practical way when it comes to our relationship with God. When we enter into His gates with thankfulness, we have a better outcome in our circumstances. When we have a thankful attitude, this shows that we respect God and have faith in Him. So, I challenge you to practice being thankful in a bad situation. The more you practice, the more you will be in control of the moment, and before you know it, it becomes a lifestyle. Being thankful doesn't just change your immediate mood or outlook; it transforms your entire approach to life, turning every obstacle into an opportunity for growth and every moment into a chance to appreciate the blessings you've been given.

Questions/Thoughts:

1. What causes you to have an ungrateful attitude? How does this equate to who God is to you?

NOTES:

_____

_____

_____

_____

_____

_____

_____

_____

Purposed

One of the most asked questions of a human being is, "Why am I here on earth? What is my purpose?" Everyone wants to know their reason for being on this earth. Everyone wants to know a reason for wanting to live. When a person doesn't know their purpose, they go on a hunt seeking out those reasons. We live in a world that teaches us to seek out purpose through vocation, through work and education. We hear that famous phrase, "You can be anything you want to be," and this is true, but in order to find our true purpose, we must seek the one who created us because He has the blueprint for our lives. The scripture tells us that God has predestined our lives and tells us that God knew us before we entered into our mothers' wombs (Jeremiah 1:5). God has planned for us to do good works. Your purpose is not just one thing; it's many things. Purpose is like a puzzle; it has many pieces to it. I believe the more mature and responsible we become as believers, the more we will live out our purpose on earth. The more we understand what we need to do and who we are in life. A parent will not give their child a car without first being of age to drive, learning all the rules about driving, and practicing how to drive. Once a parent has observed that child showing the responsibility of driving, they will feel confident enough to buy that child a car and hand over the keys. It's the same with God. He gives us gifts, talents, and abilities, and He watches to see how we will nurture them. Remember, He wants to see a return on His investment. Then God watches our character. He watches how we are going to treat people. He searches the motives of our heart. All of these things are pieces to the puzzle. Moses appointed capable men to lead, some over 10, some over 50, some over 100, and some over 1000 (Deuteronomy 1:15). The reason for this is according to what they could handle and the character they displayed to be trustworthy. Also, the scriptures tell us, "And the one whose seed was sown on the good soil, this is the man who hears the word and understands it; who indeed bears fruit and brings forth, some a hundredfold, some sixty, and some thirty" (Matthew 13:23). Though God has great things in store for us, He doesn't give it to us all at once because we have to be mature enough to handle it all. God doesn't want us to handle purpose without Him. He is the reason why we have purpose, and our lives are to bring glory to Him (Romans 11:36). I want to inform you that no parts of our lives are wasted, and God will use all of our experiences to create a purpose so great that we can't imagine it (1 Corinthians 2:9). So, I encourage you to seek out the One who can provide all the pieces to the puzzle of your life.

Questions/Thoughts:

1. Do you know what your purpose is? What pieces of the puzzle are you missing concerning your purpose?

NOTES:

_____

_____

_____

_____

_____

_____

_____

_____

_____

_____

Benediction

The word for today is "Benediction," which means to invoke a blessing, something that promotes goodness or well-being.[28] I remember hearing this word and experiencing this in church as a child. Before we would end the service, the pastor or leader would speak a benediction over the congregation. And it went something like this: "May the Lord watch between me and thee while we are absent one from another, until we meet again. Amen." Now, the benediction you heard may have been different. Did you know that the Lord told Moses to speak a benediction over Aaron and his sons? Numbers 6:22-26 (NCV) says, "May the Lord bless you and keep you. May the Lord show his kindness and have mercy on you. May the Lord watch over you and give you peace." There are so many things going on in your life and around you in the world. I'm sure with all the negativity you experience at work, at home with your family, and the things that we constantly hear on the news, you could use a benediction. As a believer in Christ, we have been given authority to speak things into our lives, and the word tells us that life and death are in the power of the tongue, and those who speak will eat the fruit of it (Proverbs 18:21 KJV). So, the bottom line is you have what you say. Yes, no matter how bad things may seem or any negative emotions you may be experiencing, you can speak great things over your life, and not only yours but also your neighbor's, your community's, and your family's. I heard a wise woman once say, "Your family is your first community." So, you can say what you want to see. I want to invoke a blessing over you today. I invoke a blessing of direction. I invoke a blessing of favor and peace upon you. Those of you who have severe anxiety, who are having racing thoughts and not getting any sleep because you are worrying about certain things, I invoke a blessing of rest upon you, in your mind, spirit, and thoughts. I declare that those negative thoughts and emotions will be silenced by God's love for you. The scripture tells us we have the authority to cast down every high thought that exalts itself against the knowledge of God (2 Corinthians 10:5). You have knowledge about

---

[28] Merriam-Webster. (n.d.). Benediction. In Merriam-Webster.com dictionary. Retrieved from https://www.merriam-webster.com/dictionary/benediction

your circumstances, debt, experiencing sickness or diseases, a wayward child, or failing relationships. But I have knowledge about God, who says that you are an overcomer (John 16:33), you don't have to worry about your life because He clothed the lilies in the field, and you are more important than those (Matthew 6:25-34). I have knowledge that this too shall pass (2 Corinthians 4:17-18). Remember, seasons change (Genesis 8; Ecclesiastes 3:1-8). This hard and difficult season you are in will pass. Lastly, I want to invoke a blessing of joy in your life. The scripture tells us that the joy of the Lord is our strength (Nehemiah 8:10). God will give you what you need in this season, and I pray that you will be aware of His presence in your life. In Jesus name, Amen!

Questions/Thoughts:

1. How can you cultivate a life that produces goodness and wellbeing?

NOTES:

_____
_____
_____
_____
_____
_____
_____
_____
_____

About the Author

Destiny is an Illinois native with two adult children and four grandchildren. Destiny discovered what she wanted to do with her life as a teenager when she was allowed to work with the intellectual and developmental disabilities (IDD) population. She found her knack for helping people while serving her community. Destiny currently resides in Tulsa, OK, has her own business, GiGi's Consulting and Social Services LLC, and is pursuing her therapist licensure.

She has an Associate Degree in Human Services from Northeast Iowa Community College (NICC), a Bachelor's Degree in Social Work from Loras College in Iowa, and a Master's Degree in Social Work from The University of Oklahoma (OU). With over 25 years of social work experience, Destiny has worked for a church in Iowa for 16 years, while working in the homeless ministry as the Homeless Director for 13 years. She also served as an intercessor, volunteering to teach and pray with women in jail for several years in Iowa.

Destiny was featured in the 2016 her magazine for women, being recognized for her community service work in Dubuque, IA. Destiny has been writing since 1997, and this is her first published book. This 52-weekly devotional book is about Destiny's life journey and how she has used her faith to help her navigate through insurmountable experiences. Destiny shares personal testimonies and stories from the Bible to uplift the readers and let them know that they are not alone during their times of adversity.

Destiny values the eight dimensions of wellness, which she believes are the keys to an individual's happiness and the enjoyment of living a fulfilled and abundant life. One of Destiny's mottos is, "If you want something new to happen in your life, do something new that will create an opportunity for something new to happen"! It is Destiny's prayer that the reader's life will be transformed in a favorable manner that will be visible to others, for their good and God's glory!

NOTES/THOUGHTS:

www.ingramcontent.com/pod-product-compliance
Lightning Source LLC
LaVergne TN
LVHW081537070526
838199LV00056B/3699